D0558691

The World Trade Organization: A Very Short Introduction

VERY SHORT INTRODUCTIONS are for anyone wanting a stimulating and accessible way in to a new subject. They are written by experts, and have been published in more than 25 languages worldwide.

The series began in 1995, and now represents a wide variety of topics in history, philosophy, religion, science, and the humanities. Over the next few years it will grow to a library of around 200 volumes – a Very Short Introduction to everything from ancient Egypt and Indian philosophy to conceptual art and cosmology.

Very Short Introductions available now:

ANARCHISM Colin Ward
ANCIENT EGYPT Ian Shaw
ANCIENT PHILOSOPHY
  Julia Annas
ANCIENT WARFARE
  Harry Sidebottom
THE ANGLO-SAXON AGE
  John Blair
ANIMAL RIGHTS David DeGrazia
ARCHAEOLOGY Paul Bahn
ARCHITECTURE
  Andrew Ballantyne
ARISTOTLE Jonathan Barnes
ART HISTORY Dana Arnold
ART THEORY Cynthia Freeland
THE HISTORY OF
  ASTRONOMY Michael Hoskin
ATHEISM Julian Baggini
AUGUSTINE Henry Chadwick
BARTHES Jonathan Culler
THE BIBLE John Riches
BRITISH POLITICS
  Anthony Wright
BUDDHA Michael Carrithers
BUDDHISM Damien Keown
BUDDHIST ETHICS Damien Keown
CAPITALISM James Fulcher
THE CELTS Barry Cunliffe
CHOICE THEORY
  Michael Allingham
CHRISTIAN ART Beth Williamson

CHRISTIANITY Linda Woodhead
CLASSICS Mary Beard and
  John Henderson
CLAUSEWITZ Michael Howard
THE COLD WAR Robert McMahon
CONSCIOUSNESS Susan Blackmore
CONTINENTAL PHILOSOPHY
  Simon Critchley
COSMOLOGY Peter Coles
CRYPTOGRAPHY
  Fred Piper and Sean Murphy
DADA AND SURREALISM
  David Hopkins
DARWIN Jonathan Howard
DEMOCRACY Bernard Crick
DESCARTES Tom Sorell
DINOSAURS David Norman
DREAMING J. Allan Hobson
DRUGS Leslie Iversen
THE EARTH Martin Redfern
EGYPTIAN MYTH
  Geraldine Pinch
EIGHTEENTH-CENTURY
  BRITAIN Paul Langford
THE ELEMENTS Philip Ball
EMOTION Dylan Evans
EMPIRE Stephen Howe
ENGELS Terrell Carver
ETHICS Simon Blackburn
THE EUROPEAN UNION
  John Pinder

EVOLUTION
  Brian and Deborah Charlesworth
FASCISM   Kevin Passmore
FOUCAULT   Gary Gutting
THE FRENCH REVOLUTION
  William Doyle
FREE WILL   Thomas Pink
FREUD   Anthony Storr
GALILEO   Stillman Drake
GANDHI   Bhikhu Parekh
GLOBALIZATION
  Manfred Steger
GLOBAL WARMING   Mark Maslin
HABERMAS
  James Gordon Finlayson
HEGEL   Peter Singer
HEIDEGGER   Michael Inwood
HIEROGLYPHS   Penelope Wilson
HINDUISM   Kim Knott
HISTORY   John H. Arnold
HOBBES   Richard Tuck
HUME   A. J. Ayer
IDEOLOGY   Michael Freeden
INDIAN PHILOSOPHY
  Sue Hamilton
INTELLIGENCE   Ian J. Deary
ISLAM   Malise Ruthven
JUDAISM   Norman Solomon
JUNG   Anthony Stevens
KAFKA   Ritchie Robertson
KANT   Roger Scruton
KIERKEGAARD   Patrick Gardiner
THE KORAN   Michael Cook
LINGUISTICS   Peter Matthews
LITERARY THEORY
  Jonathan Culler
LOCKE   John Dunn
LOGIC   Graham Priest
MACHIAVELLI   Quentin Skinner
THE MARQUIS DE SADE
  John Phillips
MARX   Peter Singer
MATHEMATICS   Timothy Gowers
MEDICAL ETHICS   Tony Hope

MEDIEVAL BRITAIN
  John Gillingham and Ralph A. Griffiths
MODERN ART   David Cottington
MODERN IRELAND   Senia Pašeta
MOLECULES   Philip Ball
MUSIC   Nicholas Cook
MYTH   Robert A. Segal
NIETZSCHE   Michael Tanner
NINETEENTH-CENTURY
  BRITAIN   Christopher Harvie and
  H. C. G. Matthew
NORTHERN IRELAND
  Marc Mulholland
PARTICLE PHYSICS   Frank Close
PAUL   E. P. Sanders
PHILOSOPHY   Edward Craig
PHILOSOPHY OF SCIENCE
  Samir Okasha
PLATO   Julia Annas
POLITICS   Kenneth Minogue
POLITICAL PHILOSOPHY
  David Miller
POSTCOLONIALISM
  Robert Young
POSTMODERNISM
  Christopher Butler
POSTSTRUCTURALISM
  Catherine Belsey
PREHISTORY   Chris Gosden
PRESOCRATIC PHILOSOPHY
  Catherine Osborne
PSYCHOLOGY   Gillian Butler and
  Freda McManus
QUANTUM THEORY
  John Polkinghorne
RENAISSANCE ART
  Geraldine A. Johnson
ROMAN BRITAIN   Peter Salway
ROUSSEAU   Robert Wokler
RUSSELL   A. C. Grayling
RUSSIAN LITERATURE
  Catriona Kelly
THE RUSSIAN REVOLUTION
  S. A. Smith

SCHIZOPHRENIA
  Chris Frith and Eve Johnstone
SCHOPENHAUER
  Christopher Janaway
SHAKESPEARE   Germaine Greer
SOCIAL AND CULTURAL
  ANTHROPOLOGY
  John Monaghan and Peter Just
SOCIALISM   Michael Newman
SOCIOLOGY   Steve Bruce
SOCRATES   C. C. W. Taylor
THE SPANISH CIVIL WAR
  Helen Graham
SPINOZA   Roger Scruton

STUART BRITAIN
  John Morrill
TERRORISM   Charles Townshend
THEOLOGY   David F. Ford
THE HISTORY OF TIME
  Leofranc Holford-Strevens
THE TUDORS   John Guy
TWENTIETH-CENTURY
  BRITAIN   Kenneth O. Morgan
WITTGENSTEIN   A. C. Grayling
WORLD MUSIC   Philip Bohlman
THE WORLD TRADE
  ORGANIZATION
  Amrita Narlikar

Available soon:

AFRICAN HISTORY
  John Parker and
  Richard Rathbone
THE BRAIN   Michael O'Shea
CHAOS   Leonard Smith
CITIZENSHIP   Richard Bellamy
CLASSICAL ARCHITECTURE
  Robert Tavernor
CONTEMPORARY ART
  Julian Stallabrass
THE CRUSADES
  Christopher Tyerman
THE DEAD SEA SCROLLS
  Timothy Lim
DERRIDA   Simon Glendinning
DESIGN   John Heskett
ECONOMICS   Partha Dasgupta
THE END OF THE WORLD
  Bill McGuire
EXISTENTIALISM   Thomas Flynn
FEMINISM   Margaret Walters
THE FIRST WORLD WAR
  Michael Howard
FOSSILS   Keith Thomson

FUNDAMENTALISM
  Malise Ruthven
HUMAN EVOLUTION
  Bernard Wood
INTERNATIONAL RELATIONS
  Paul Wilkinson
JAZZ   Brian Morton
JOURNALISM   Ian Hargreaves
MANDELA   Tom Lodge
THE MIND   Martin Davies
NATIONALISM   Steven Grosby
PERCEPTION   Richard Gregory
PHILOSOPHY OF RELIGION
  Jack Copeland and Diane Proudfoot
PHOTOGRAPHY   Steve Edwards
RACISM   Ali Rattansi
THE RAJ   Denis Judd
THE RENAISSANCE   Jerry Brotton
ROMAN EMPIRE
  Christopher Kelly
SARTRE   Christina Howells
SIKHISM   Eleanor Nesbitt
TRAGEDY   Adrian Poole
THE VIKINGS   Julian Richards

For more information visit our web site

www.oup.co.uk/vsi/

Amrita Narlikar

THE
WORLD TRADE
ORGANIZATION

A Very Short Introduction

OXFORD

UNIVERSITY PRESS

Great Clarendon Street, Oxford OX2 6DP

Oxford University Press is a department of the University of Oxford.
It furthers the University's objective of excellence in research, scholarship,
and education by publishing worldwide in

Oxford New York

Auckland Cape Town Dar es Salaam Hong Kong Karachi
Kuala Lumpur Madrid Melbourne Mexico City Nairobi
New Delhi Shanghai Taipei Toronto

With offices in

Argentina Austria Brazil Chile Czech Republic France Greece
Guatemala Hungary Italy Japan Poland Portugal Singapore
South Korea Switzerland Thailand Turkey Ukraine Vietnam

Oxford is a registered trade mark of Oxford University Press
in the UK and in certain other countries

Published in the United States
by Oxford University Press Inc., New York

British Library Cataloguing in Publication Data

Data available

Library of Congress Cataloging in Publication Data

Data available

ISBN 0-19-280608-4
978-0-19-280608-6

1 3 5 7 9 10 8 6 4 2

Typeset by RefineCatch Ltd, Bungay, Suffolk
Printed in Great Britain by
TJ International Ltd, Padstow, Cornwall

To Amba Devi of Kolhapur

Contents

Preface   xi

Acknowledgements   xiv

Abbreviations   xvii

List of illustrations   xix

List of tables   xx

1   Who needs an international trade organization?   1

2   The creation of the World Trade Organization   22

3   Decision-making and negotiation processes   42

4   The expanding mandate   59

5   Settling disputes   85

6   The Doha Development Agenda   99

7   The burden of governance   122

Further reading   139

Index   145

Preface

For an apparently small organization dealing with abstruse trade matters in Geneva, the World Trade Organization (WTO) arouses surprising levels of popular interest, emotions, and high drama. At the last high-level meeting of the WTO at Cancun in 2003, non-governmental organizations staged massive anti-WTO demonstrations, participating countries threatened to walk out of the conference, and a South Korean farmer committed suicide to show just what he thought of the WTO's rules on agriculture. Nor was Cancun unusual in any way; most ministerial-level meetings of the organization have come to be associated with impassioned protests and angry mobs.

There is no dearth of books and research papers that offer detailed economic and legal explanations and interpretations of the agreements of the WTO. There are also many papers written by civil society activists – some less judiciously researched than others – for the purposes of policy advocacy. But analyses that focus on the *politics* of the WTO are rare to find. This book seeks to fill this gap in the literature, and tries to get to the heart of the WTO as an international organization and the politics that underlie its origins, functioning, and evolution.

Two features of this book are worth highlighting. First, my central approach to the study of the WTO as an international institution is through the lens of negotiation process. By analysing the constant interplay between existing structures and underlying processes, I present an account of not only the initial bargain that led to the creation of the WTO but also how the organization has evolved in terms of its membership, mandate, and everyday functioning. Contingency, path dependence, and negotiation process go a long way in determining how the WTO has got to the point it has, rather than rational design of the institution. Second, developing countries form an integral part of the story presented here. This attention to developing countries is not one that I had initially intended. But all my research findings continuously pointed in a direction that has been largely neglected: the link between power asymmetries and international institutions. I found that power differences between developed and developing countries played a crucial role in the making and shaping of the WTO, and that the institution itself affects power discrepancies in many different ways. As a result, power, marginalization, discontent, and development are recurring themes in this book.

I have also chosen to engage directly with the many public debates on the WTO. The organization presents a fascinating mix of contradictions. It is, by far, the smallest and youngest of the three international economic organizations (the other two being the International Monetary Fund and the World Bank). But it makes rules that often encroach into areas that have traditionally lain within the domestic jurisdictions of states, and with which all 147 members must comply. It is true that many of the WTO's activities lie in the obscure and esoteric realms of trade policy. But the deep and far-reaching impact of its rules on the everyday lives of peoples means that it is not an institution of interest to economists alone. On paper, the WTO has the most democratic procedures of the three economic organizations; in practice, the WTO has come under immense criticism for its almost 'English club atmosphere' and exclusionary meetings. The WTO is simultaneously accused, in broadsheets and elsewhere, of not doing enough and of doing too much: some argue that the WTO should cover issues of labour, gender, and development, while others view its already expansionist tendencies with alarm. Contradictory proposals for institutional reform abound. The WTO is adored by some, and vilified by many. By presenting an account and explanation of the evolution, purpose, and political workings of the WTO, it is hoped that this book will help the reader to better navigate the murky waters of international trade politics.

Acknowledgements

While conducting research for this book, I have relied extensively on interviews with trade negotiators and international bureaucrats from the United Nations Conference on Trade and Development and the World Trade Organization. They are too numerous to name here, and many sought anonymity for obvious reasons. I am extremely grateful to them for so generously sharing their experiences and concerns with me.

I owe a special debt of gratitude to John Odell and Diana Tussie for many long and inspiring conversations about trade politics over the years. Their guidance has had a long-lasting and invaluable impact on my research, and every discussion with them has been as enjoyable as it has been enlightening and memorable.

I am equally indebted to Andrew Hurrell and Desmond King for many stimulating questions and ideas that we explored together in the pleasant environs of Nuffield College; without their intellectual support and encouragement, this project might not have come through.

Colleagues and friends contributed to the book in crucial ways, reading and commenting on the manuscript (or parts thereof), engaging in fruitful exchanges on the subject, and providing moral support. In particular, I would like to thank Ewan Harrison,

Konrad Banaszek, Theo Farrell, Steve McGuire, and Mette-Eilstrup Sangiovanni.

Alan Renwick gave the book a running start and then stood by me throughout, providing detailed and constructive suggestions on the manuscript.

I am thankful to all the institutions that supported this project. The Nuffield Foundation funded my research leave, and I am especially grateful to the trustees and Louie Burghes for their constant interest and support. Library facilities at the Bodleian were critical in the early stages of the project, as was my research affiliation with the Centre for International Studies, University of Oxford. Excellent infrastructure and supportive colleagues at the Centre for International Studies in Cambridge and at Newnham College provided the ideal milieu for its completion. Here, a special note of thanks is extended to Chris Hill, Onora O'Neill, and Terri Apter.

The editor of the series, Marsha Filion, who carefully and patiently shepherded the project from the beginning to its completion, deserves my warmest appreciation. I thank her and her colleagues at Oxford University Press, particularly James Thompson, who worked long and hard and with great efficiency to keep to the tight schedule. The original proposal and manuscript benefited from the comments of three anonymous referees.

For their friendship and loyalty, I would like to thank my 'English parents' Linda and Moreton Moore, and also David Armstrong, Maggie Armstrong, Caroline Lombardo, John Love, Rachel Muers, Mathan Satchithananthan, and Ed Tarte.

My greatest debt is to my parents, Aruna and Anant Narlikar. Anant, who normally studies low-temperature physics, was equally adept in providing insightful comments about the high temperatures that have surrounded trade politics. Aruna, despite her busy schedule, found time to share new ideas, raise incisive questions, read several drafts and re-drafts, and provide comments that helped me immensely in writing this book. This book could not have been written without their critical comments and constant encouragement.

The memory of my friend Batasha has been a constant source of inspiration.

The responsibility for any errors in the book lies with the author alone.

Abbreviations

AD	Anti-Dumping
AMS	Aggregate Measure of Support
ATC	Agreement on Textiles and Clothing
CAP	Common Agricultural Policy (of Europe)
CVD	Countervailing Duty
DDA	Doha Development Agenda
DSB	Dispute Settlement Body
DSM	Dispute Settlement Mechanism
DSU	Dispute Settlement Understanding
ECOSOC	Economic and Social Council
GATS	General Agreement on Trade in Services
GATT	General Agreement on Tariffs and Trade
HOD	Heads of delegations
ICITO	Interim Commission for the International Trade Organization
IMF	International Monetary Fund
IPRs	Intellectual Property Rights
ITO	International Trade Organization
LDC	Least Developed Country
LMG	Like-Minded Group
MFN	Most Favoured Nation
NAMA	Non-Agricultural Market Access

NGO	Non-Governmental Organization
NTB	Non-Tariff Barrier
PSP	Principal Supplier Principle
QRs	Quantitative Restrictions
S&D	Special and Differential (treatment)
SPS	Sanitary and Phytosanitary (measures)
TBT	Technical Barriers to Trade
TNC	Trade Negotiations Committee
TPRM	Trade Policy Review Mechanism
TRIMs	Trade-Related Investment Measures
TRIPs	Trade-Related Intellectual Property Rights
TRQ	Tariff Rate Quota
UN	United Nations
UNCTAD	United Nations Conference on Trade and Development
VERs	Voluntary Export Restraints
WIPO	World Intellectual Property Organization

List of illustrations

1 Anti-WTO
demonstration,
Seattle, 1999   1
© Steven Rubin/The Image
Works/TopFoto.co.uk

2 Bretton Woods
conference, 1944   11
© United Nations Photo
Library

3 Signing of the Marrakesh
agreement   26
© World Trade Organization

4 Aerial view of the WTO
building   27
© Lightmotif/Blatt

5 WTO logo   31
© World Trade Organization

6 Renato Ruggiero
becomes
Director-General, May
1995   34
© World Trade Organization

7 Organizational
structure of the WTO   38
© World Trade Organization

8 Animal conference   44
© Les Barton/Cartoonstock.com

9 Copyright cartoon   83
© Andres Soria/
Cartoonstock.com

10 Anti-WTO demonstration
in Seattle   101
© Steven Rubin/The Image
Works/TopFoto.co.uk

11 Trade Justice Movement
demonstration in
Trafalgar Square,
November 2001   117
© Dave Thomson

12 'Democracy versus
WTO' protest flag   123
© STR/Reuters

13 WTO cartoon   133
     © Chappatte in *Le Temps*/
     www.globecartoon.com

The publisher and the author apologize for any errors or omissions in the above list. If contacted they will be pleased to rectify these at the earliest opportunity.

List of tables

1   Trade rounds in the GATT   20
     © World Trade Organization

2   Structure of the WTO agreements   61

3   Stages in the dispute settlement process   88

Chapter 1
Who needs an international trade organization?

For a relatively youthful organization concerned with esoteric trade affairs, the WTO has already aroused unprecedented fury and passion. The extent to which controversies about the WTO have entered into the public domain was most graphically illustrated in the popular demonstrations at the Seattle meeting in 1999 (see Figure 1).

At the Cancun meeting in 2003, these passions showed little sign of abating. Given the anger the WTO has generated, in this chapter we

1. Public discontent and dissatisfaction against the WTO came to the fore at the Seattle Ministerial Conference in 1999

ask the question: who needs an international trade organization anyway?

Is there a case for an international trade organization?

To make a case for or against an international trade organization, we need to identify the role that such an institution might be expected to play in the global economic system. The Agreement establishing the WTO commits its member states to a variety of noble objectives: improved standards of living, full employment, expanded production of and trade in goods and services, sustainable development, and an enhanced share of developing countries in world trade. The Agreement further commits its members to contribute to these objectives 'by entering into reciprocal and mutually advantageous arrangements directed to the substantial reduction of tariffs and other barriers to trade and to the elimination of discriminatory treatment in international trade relations'. The WTO as an institution is clearly committed to trade liberalization. It is worth emphasizing that this commitment is not an end in itself, but is seen as a means to achieving the broader social ends mentioned above.

Barring a few qualifications, economists view the commitment to trade liberalization as a welfare-maximizing pursuit. Economic theory since the middle of the 18th century has presented the advantages in lowering tariffs for most parties in most situations. The gains from trade derive from specialization on the basis of comparative advantage. Put very simply, if each country were to produce that which it is best at producing (in comparison to all the other products that it could still produce but with lesser efficiency), there would be a bigger output of each of these efficiently produced products in each country. The countries could then trade among themselves, with each exporting the good or service in which it has the comparative advantage and importing the good or service in which it has a comparative disadvantage. Such an exchange would benefit all the countries involved. In fact, as per classical trade theory, the gains from trade accrue to any country that lowers trade barriers irrespective of what other countries do, thereby suggesting that the rational actor may be expected to pursue unilateral trade liberalization. Indeed, as Paul Krugman puts it: 'If economists ruled the world, there would be no need for a World Trade Organization.'

A quick peek into the real world suggests that despite the promise of free trade, countries have historically been reluctant to reduce trade barriers and quick to raise them. A frequently cited example of this policy inclination, and its disastrous consequences, is that of the United States and other countries in the years of the Great Depression. Following the stock market crash of 1929, the US Congress adopted the Smoot-Hawley Tariff Act in 1930 that raised US tariffs to an average of nearly 60%. Most of the major trade partners of the US retaliated by raising similar tariff barriers and engaging in a competitive devaluation of their currencies. Prices fell further, tariff barriers went up, and a race to the bottom ensued that worsened the Great Depression. The cataclysmic effects of these beggar-thy-neighbour policies of the 1930s left a long-lasting impression on the minds of policy-makers in the post-war years. It was recognized that cooperation among states is difficult to organize or sustain without the presence of international institutions, even if states are aware that non-cooperation will adversely affect all parties.

There are several reasons – economic and political – why states act in ways that turn out to be detrimental to their self-interest. The first insight on why some states may choose the path of protectionism, despite the benefits of trade liberalization, comes directly from economic theory and the notion of the 'optimal tariff'. While it is unambiguously in the interest of the small country to liberalize trade, economic theory tells us that the situation is different for large countries. The optimal tariff argument tells us that it may be in the interest of a large country to restrict trade at a certain 'optimal' level, as it will be able to change the terms of trade in its favour by so doing. Should the large state intervene unilaterally and solely in its foreign trade relations, it would incur gains at the cost of other producers and consumers abroad. Such restrictions would hence translate into reduced welfare for the world as a whole, though they would work to the advantage of the large state concerned. However, as the example of the Smoot-Hawley tariffs in the US showed, other states are unlikely to accept such restrictions passively and would impose similar, retaliatory restrictions. The result would be a downward spiral in the welfare of all states caught in the tariff war. Economists Bernard Hoekman and Michel Kostecki provide a succinct interpretation of this problem in terms of the classic Prisoners' Dilemma game: 'it is in each country's interest to impose restrictions, but the result of such individually rational policies is inefficient.'

What would the impact of such a tariff war among large states be on smaller countries? The African saying 'When two elephants fight, it is the grass that gets trampled' applies well in this context. High tariffs, targeted specifically between the US and the EU, for instance, might at first glance imply that small countries find these vast markets opened up to them without the competition of the giants. But the race to reach these large markets would draw the small countries too into a war of their own, involving unsustainable price-cutting and an expensive race to the bottom. As a result, a tariff war between the larger states would result in reduced world welfare and adversely affect both large and small countries.

The Prisoners' Dilemma problem in international trade is well known, and governments recognize the costs of retaliation that they risk if any one of them imposes trade restrictions. But there is still no guarantee that one renegade and powerful state will not resort to this individually rational but collectively sub-optimal outcome, thereby dragging all the other states into a chain reaction of retaliations. Equally plausible is the danger that one (or more) state may withdraw from its commitments to trade liberalization, imposing unexpected and heavy costs on its trading partners. The plausibility of these risks often acts as a deterrent for most states from committing to trade liberalization. The best way of preventing such a mutually destructive situation from emerging is by ensuring that countries commit to trade liberalization on a reciprocal basis. Reciprocal trade liberalization increases the gains from trade by further expanding the output to be traded. But more importantly, if countries have some mechanism of binding themselves and each other to commitments on tariff reductions, the risk of a retaliatory trade war (akin to the 1930s trade war) is reduced. Herein lies the logic of multilateral trade liberalization. An international trade organization establishes rules of reciprocity on a generalized basis across three or more countries, and thereby multilateralizes reciprocity. By monitoring and enforcing these rules, the multilateral trade organization guards against cheating and defection by member countries. Indeed, the *raison d'être* for most international organizations across most issue-areas lies in a similar logic.

Besides facilitating international cooperation, institutionalized rules of reciprocity, monitoring. and enforcement in a multilateral trade organization also offer some important political advantages to member governments. Trade liberalization may improve overall national welfare, but it also entails disruptive distributive consequences within societies by producing losers and gainers. Political economists have pointed out that the greatest losses from liberalization accrue to import-competing industries, whereas the biggest gains accrue to consumers. One might expect the consumer interests gaining from the liberalization to balance out against the protectionist producer interests that stand to lose. But the problem with such a distribution is that producer interests tend to be far more concentrated, organized, and vocal than consumer interests. Multilateral liberalization opens up several foreign markets and thereby ensures that domestic firms seeking foreign market access will balance out against the protectionist firms. The process of trade liberalization becomes not only economically beneficial but also politically feasible.

Adherence to the rules of an international trade organization also serves an important domestic imperative for governments by allowing them to resist protectionist demands. When faced with such pressures, particularly when the going gets tough and interest groups are demanding a reversal of liberal policies, governments can claim that their hands are tied by appealing to the international codes of conduct of the organization with which they are bound. The fact that the particular government had taken on its liberalization programme within the auspices of a multilateral trade organization means that reneging on those commitments will have punitive consequences of various types. Depending on the nature of the organization and its enforcement mechanism, these consequences could range from international disapproval, to compensating all the members for the costs they incur as a result of the particular country's action, to direct retaliation. Indeed, governments frequently appeal to such rationales to justify unpopular actions that are supposed to have longer-term benefits (and not simply in trade matters) by claiming that their international commitments bind them to act thus. It is not surprising that across developing countries, many of the programmes of economic reform and restructuring in the late 1980s to early 1990s, particularly those involving some difficult distributive consequences, were taken on in the shadow of the international economic organizations.

All the benefits of having an international trade organization noted so far apply to countries irrespective of their economic size and bargaining power. But developing countries have an additional set of stakes in the existence of such an organization (see box). It is now a generally accepted argument in international relations theory, first put forth by Stephen Krasner in 1985, that weak states seek rules-based, authoritative international regimes. Such regimes introduce a greater measure of certainty in international relations and thereby help mitigate a rampant abuse of power by stronger states. This certainty is a valuable resource for developing countries, which have limited resources and can put them to better use if the rules of the game are established. The regulation of international trade through a multilateral trade organization further provides developing countries one of the few safeguards that they have against arbitrary arm-twisting by the powerful. Unlike in a bilateral context, developed countries cannot easily renege on their commitments in a multilateral institution; if they do so, they must face the penalties that follow from breaking international rules. And finally, the existence of a multilateral trade organization provides developing countries with an important institutional context within which they can build coalitions and thereby improve their bargaining position. As a result, developing countries tend to prefer more defined rules, and greater enforcement capacity in the institution administering those rules (with the caveat, of course, that much depends on the nature of the rules and who actually administers them). A multilateral trade organization can present the most rigorous codification of rules. It may be safe to say that, especially if a country is small and weak, its international economic life without an international trade organization would be 'nasty, brutish, and short'.

Defining developing countries

For many years now, academics have been engaged in a debate on the concept of the developing world. Many have argued that the concept has been rendered obsolete due to the increasing differentiation among developing countries. Indeed, the vulnerabilities of the small economies of the Caribbean, with their proximity to the US, are very different from the threats faced by the smaller economies of Africa or the Pacific, let alone their divergence from the emerging powers of the developing world such as Brazil, China, and India. However, these differences notwithstanding, developing countries share two sets of characteristics – marginalization or peripherality, and 'Third World schizophrenia'.

Marginalization, or peripherality, refers to the inability of developing countries to shape international institutions to their advantage or emerge as full players in the international system. Due to domestic and international weaknesses, often derived from their colonial past, these countries find themselves in the position of rule-takers rather than agenda-setters. This is as true of countries like Brazil and India, which have traditionally been invited to the negotiating table but nonetheless have repeatedly complained that their concerns are disregarded, as it is of the smaller developing countries that have found it difficult to get a place in key decision-making meetings.

Related to marginalization is the phenomenon that Mohammed Ayoob succinctly terms 'Third World schizophrenia'. As the intruder majority in a system of states that was not built to suit their advantage, developing countries have sought to bring about systemic change. But as a result of their vulnerabilities, they also have an incentive to preserve the existing system of rules that provides legitimacy to their statehood and ensures their very survival.

The shared features of marginalization and schizophrenia impair the bargaining skill and resolve of developing countries. These characteristics are not confined to the smallest and the poorest developing countries; rich developing countries (such as the Southeast Asian economies even prior to the Asian financial crisis) and large developing countries with regional clout (such as Brazil and India) share the trait of limited bargaining power. The group of countries sharing these features are often collectively referred to as the South (in contrast to the developed countries, the North), the Third World, or the developing world.

Belonging to the developing world is at least as much a product of self-designation by the countries concerned and recognition by other members of the group, as it is of any objective criteria applied by outsiders. In keeping with this, most international organizations leave the task of claiming developing country status to the countries themselves. Often, this is a matter of negotiation between the particular country and other countries that will be affected by the decision. For instance, this proved to be a bone of contention in China's negotiations for accession to the WTO. China claimed developing country status, which would allow it to use special provisions reserved for developing countries, such as longer transition periods in the implementation of certain rules. Developed countries baulked at the idea. A compromise was finally arrived at, but only after long and protracted negotiation.

Note that within the developing world is a sub-group of countries, referred to as the Least Developed Countries (LDCs). Unlike the term 'developing country', which is intersubjectively defined, LDCs are countries identified by the UN that meet all three criteria of low income (currently marked at below $750 gross domestic product per capita), human resource weakness, and economic vulnerability. In 2003, Senegal was added to the list of LDCs, making a total of 50 countries.

Modelling a multilateral trade organization: the ITO and the GATT

While the previous section has argued strongly in favour of a multilateral trade organization, this does not amount to a defence of the World Trade Organization. An international organization can take a variety of shapes, and may be guided by a spectrum of rules that have far-reaching implications for international power and wealth distributions. In this section, we briefly examine two models of a multilateral trade organization that were formulated by international negotiators: one that never actually materialized and one that did.

The International Trade Organization (ITO)

Following the end of the Second World War, international leaders were anxious to build safeguards and institutions into the international system that would protect the world from the recurrence of such disastrous events. The US took the lead in advancing the view that free trade provided an important mechanism for achieving world peace. US Secretary of State, Cordell Hull, was an eminent and influential exponent of this view:

> I have never faltered, and I will never falter, in my belief that enduring peace and the welfare of nations are indissolubly connected with friendliness, fairness, equality and the maximum practicable degree of freedom in international trade.

Cordell Hull, *Economic Barriers to Peace* (New York: Woodrow Wilson Foundation, 1937, p. 14)

The Allies, particularly the US and Britain, began discussions about the reconstruction of the world economic order even before the war effort was over. In 1944, at the Bretton Woods conference, the US and Britain signed an agreement that provided the blueprint for the post-war economy. Three pillars were envisaged for the purpose of maintaining international economic cooperation: the International Monetary Fund (IMF), the International Bank for Reconstruction and Development (or the World Bank), and the International Trade Organization (ITO). Following the bilateral trade negotiations between the US and Britain, successive multilateral conferences were held between 1946 and 1948. The outcome of this process was the Havana Charter, the draft agreement for the creation of the

2. **Participants at the United Nations Monetary and Financial Conference at Mount Washington Hotel in Bretton Woods in 1944, which led to the creation of the International Monetary Fund and the World Bank**

ITO, which was signed by 53 of the 56 countries participating in the conference.

Despite this promising multilateral commitment, the ITO never came into existence. The agreement required ratification in the US Congress before it could be implemented, and no other country was willing to commit to the rules of an ITO without the US aboard. But US ratification proved to be problematic, despite its leading role in the genesis and evolution of the idea of the ITO. By 1948, the context that had initially led to the idea of the ITO had changed substantially. Domestically in the US, it began to appear extremely unlikely that the Republican Congress of 1948 would ratify the Charter despite the support that the Havana process had enjoyed from the Democratic presidency. International imperatives further demanded that the attention of the Congress be devoted to more immediate and pressing matters. Finally, in 1950, President Truman announced that he would not be submitting the Charter to the Congress for ratification. Given the preponderance of the US in the post-war economy, other countries decided that an ITO without the participation of the US would be meaningless. Richard Gardner's words about the 'ignominious fate' of the ITO resonate here: 'It did not have a chance to die: it was simply stillborn.' This outcome cannot be understood without a brief examination of the content of the Havana Charter. Within the expanse of its mandate and the details of its organization lay the seeds of its failure.

The ITO envisaged by the Havana Charter had a far-reaching mandate, and an elaborate organization to implement it. This expansive mandate was very much a product of the post-war context. The liberalizing ITO was charged with the tasks of solving many of the problems that we see today as belonging inside the borders of states, but which were especially serious concerns in the post-war years. Hence, besides covering the obvious area of commercial policy, the 106 articles of the ITO extended to areas of employment, economic development, restrictive business practices, and commodity agreements. It gave recognition to the importance of ensuring fair labour standards, and also incorporated provisions that allowed governments to address their development and humanitarian concerns.

The Havana Charter endowed the ITO with a detailed organizational structure to implement its mandate. It was envisaged explicitly as a specialized agency of the United Nations. The articles provided detailed prescriptions regarding decision-making procedures. They also provided for the creation of an Executive Board of 18 members, to be voted for by two-thirds majority, with 8 places reserved for member countries 'of chief economic importance'. Commissions would be created to perform the functions of the organization, which were to be appointed by the Executive Board and also report back to the Board. The Charter also gave the ITO the power of rule enforcement by building a clear dispute settlement process within it. In the event of a dispute, affected members were first required to consult among themselves. The matter could then be taken to the Executive Board, which could arrive at a decision by majority vote. The Board could also refer the matter to the plenary conference of the ITO. Further, any member affected and dissatisfied by a decision of the Conference could refer the matter to the International Court of Justice.

Unfortunately, by logrolling the diverse and often contradictory demands of all potential members of the ITO, the negotiators of the Havana Charter ended up with a final package that satisfied no one. The process for negotiating the Charter had, as its starting point, the US view that free trade was the remedy for a variety of post-war problems, including unemployment and economic instability. But in response to the war-torn economies of Western Europe, and particularly as a result of pressure from Keynesian Britain, the Charter also provided for detailed exceptions to this principle. As a result of British pressure, the Charter accepted the system of imperial preferences and provided escape clauses for countries experiencing balance of payment difficulties.

Trade-offs between the Americans and the British underlay the greater part of the negotiation process for the Havana Charter, until the London Conference in 1946. In London, however, developing countries (led particularly by Brazil, Chile, and India) disrupted the cosy consensus and demanded that the Charter include exceptions that allowed them to impose special quantitative and other restrictions to facilitate their economic development. These countries were successful, and many of their demands were incorporated into the development provisions of the Charter, including a special section that identified economic development as a central objective of the ITO. But the absence of these interlocutors from the negotiation table when the idea of the ITO was conceived meant that their demands were not fully integrated into the text. They formed important additions to the document, and the list of exceptions in the Charter grew.

Domestic constituencies within the US also ensured that exceptions were built into the broader commitment to free trade. Hence, for instance, the Department of Agriculture managed to secure an exception on quantitative restrictions and export subsidies so that US agricultural policies remained largely untouched by the ITO. The mix of commitments that resulted was contradictory, volatile, and unsustainable. Within the US, the Charter was severely denounced by, to use William Diebold's terms, the 'perfectionists' and the 'protectionists' alike. For the perfectionists, the Charter comprised nothing but exceptions, and did not go far enough in removing the trade barriers of other countries. The protectionists, in turn, pointed to the adverse effects of higher low-cost imports. Interestingly, the ITO debate catalysed an unholy alliance of sorts between the perfectionists and the protectionists, with these traditionally opposed groups conveniently converging in their denunciation of the ITO for allowing too much scope for government controls and escape mechanisms for foreign economies. Faced with such opposition, the possibility that the Congress would agree to ratify the Havana Charter was slim. It is unsurprising that the ITO died before it was born.

The failures of the ITO negotiation process struck deep. The ITO had collapsed under the weight of its own ambitions. It taught trade negotiators and their political masters some important lessons about the reach that a multilateral trade organization could politically achieve at the time. It illustrated that any multilateral process risks derailment if it does not take into account the views of affected constituencies, whether they are domestic interests or smaller countries at the negotiating table. As we will see later in the book, the lessons of the ITO experiment have acquired even greater resonance today, when the WTO is beleaguered by demands that it expand its regulation into domestic issues such as labour and the environment. More immediately after its demise and with far-reaching consequences that extend to the present day, the failures of the ITO experiment helped negotiators identify the politically feasible. This political feasibility was to be found in the General Agreement on Tariffs and Trade.

The General Agreement on Tariffs and Trade (GATT)

As early as 1945, when discussions for the ITO were underway, the US proposed that a multilateral commercial treaty on tariff reductions be negotiated among the participating countries. The rationale behind this proposal was the recognition by the US administration that though an ITO (being a multilateral *organization*) would need ratification by the Congress, a trade agreement could be negotiated and implemented more easily under the authority granted to the Executive by the 1945 Reciprocal Trade Agreements Act. Simultaneously with the negotiations on the Havana Charter, negotiations on a multilateral tariff-reduction treaty entered into full swing at the Geneva Conference in 1947. The result of the latter set of negotiations was the General Agreement on Tariffs and Trade (GATT). This was to serve as an interim agreement until the ITO came into force, and covered issues that were to be included in the Commercial Policy chapter (Chapter IV) of the Havana Charter. It was signed accordingly by 23 countries, 11 of which were developing countries, in January 1948 and was to provide a provisional basis for multilateral cooperation until the ITO was formed. This temporary agreement provided the basis for the international trading system for 47 years.

The coverage of the GATT was minuscule in comparison to the far more ambitious ITO; in fact, it was no more than the commercial policy chapter of the ITO with a weak dispute settlement mechanism. The original document made no mention of employment, development, restrictive business practices, or commodity agreements, let alone covering issues such as labour standards. Unlike the Havana Charter, which extended to domestic constituencies through its rules on the monopolistic practices of firms, the GATT applied only to governments. Its mandate stood firmly outside of the boundaries of states and dealt only with tariff barriers. Part I of the agreement established the principle of non-discrimination by requiring that all contracting parties accord Most Favoured Nation (MFN) status to each other (though exceptions such as imperial preferences and regional agreements were permitted). It also included the schedules of tariff concessions. Part III covered procedural aspects, including accessions, amendments, and withdrawals. The substantive obligations were included in Part II. But as the GATT had been agreed to only on a provisional basis, the Protocol of Provisional Application allowed an important exception for the implementation of Part II. As per this protocol, signatory governments were required to apply Part II only 'to the fullest extent not inconsistent with existing legislation'. This meant that contracting parties could claim 'grandfather rights' for any pre-existing legislation and would not be required to implement the particular GATT rule.

If the coverage of the GATT presents a striking contrast to the ITO model, perhaps even more interesting was its legal nature. The GATT was little more than a negotiating forum, held together by a multilateral treaty signed by contracting parties (rather than members of an organization). To refer to joint action by the members acting as a collective body, the term 'CONTRACTING PARTIES' (in the upper case) was used, as opposed to 'organization' or even 'membership'. GATT analyst Gilbert Winham has described it as a 'formally-contracted, rule-oriented, non-organizational form of cooperation in international affairs'. The GATT lacked the legal personality that international organizations enjoy, and it could not authorize collective action against individual countries.

This primarily contractual rather than organizational character of the GATT had some important practical implications for its everyday functioning. Initially, the contracting parties would meet once or twice annually, but in 1951 an inter-sessional committee was formed specifically to organize airmail or telegraphic ballots to vote on certain kinds of import restrictions. This was replaced by a Council of Representatives in 1960. Again emphasizing its provisional nature, the GATT Secretariat was known as the Interim

Commission for the International Trade Organization (ICITO). All GATT proceedings were driven by the contracting parties, in which the role of the Secretariat was minimal. Its dispute settlement mechanism was also weak. It eventually evolved from a working party of nations that provided a ruling in the early GATT years to a panel of experts. But all panel reports had to be adopted by the CONTRACTING PARTIES through consensus, and the losing party could (and did) block or delay this adoption process.

In terms of actual decision-making, the agreement entitled each contracting party to one vote. Article XXV.5 further stated, 'Except as otherwise provided for in this Agreement, decisions of the CONTRACTING PARTIES will be taken by a majority of votes cast.' In practice, however, the GATT evolved the norm of decision-making by consensus; that is, a decision would be arrived at if none of the parties present objected to it. These decisions were usually reached in the so-called Green Room meetings, which worked by invitation only. Tariff negotiations were conducted primarily on the Principal Supplier Principle: the principal suppliers and consumers of a particular product would negotiate tariff reductions and then extend the concessions to all contracting parties.

The result of this non-existent organizational structure of the GATT was that adherence to it was less expensive than would have been the case for the ITO. Given these minimal costs of participation, particularly for developed countries, it is not surprising that the GATT survived for as long as it did. But the weakness of the institution also meant that it did little to address the power asymmetries that severely disadvantaged developing countries in their trade relations. The onus of negotiating and implementing agreements fell on the members themselves, with little help from the Secretariat. Developing countries found themselves ill-equipped to participate effectively in this theoretically one-member-one-vote treaty due to their limited technical capacity. They found themselves further handicapped as they were excluded from the key decision-making consultations that took place in the

Green Room (the exceptions were Brazil and India, which were original members of the GATT and regular invitees to the Green Room meetings). These limitations of process were important in themselves in creating a feeling of marginalization from the GATT among its weakest members. But they also translated into the substance of the GATT, with adverse outcomes for developing countries.

The Principal Supplier Principle was one negotiating process that resulted in the automatic exclusion of developing countries from the agenda-setting process, and developed countries were able to pack the agenda with issues of interest to themselves. Admittedly, the concessions negotiated through the Principal Supplier Principle were extended to all the other contracting parties, but often these concessions were on products in which developing countries lacked an export advantage. Products that mattered as significant exports from developing countries were excluded from the mandate of the GATT through a variety of exceptions. The most infamous of these were agriculture and textiles. The GATT had previously permitted quotas and export subsidies on agricultural products. These rules on agriculture were further weakened and special waivers added to allow non-tariff barriers and quantitative restrictions. The US was the first to make use of such a waiver in 1955; the GATT agricultural regime was in fact sufficiently loose even to permit the existence of Europe's Common Agricultural Policy. In the case of textiles, with the accession of Japan in 1955, domestic industries in several developed countries demanded the right to impose import restrictions on cheap textile exports from Japan. A variety of techniques were used to enable this protectionism, including the use of 'Voluntary Export Restraints' from the exporting countries. This protectionist regime eventually crystallized into the Multi-Fibre Agreement of 1974.

Finally, development concerns that had been incorporated into the Havana Charter were non-existent in the original GATT. Part IV on Trade and Development was added on to the GATT in 1965 after some intense lobbying by developing countries within the GATT, the UN General Assembly, and the United Nations Conference on Trade and Development (UNCTAD). It recognized the principle of non-reciprocity, but its language was weak and it delivered few concrete measures to address development-related concerns. Given these procedural and substantive weaknesses of the GATT as an international institution, developing countries were quick to dismiss it as a 'rich man's club' and sought alternative forums such as the General Assembly and the UNCTAD to enunciate their demands.

The dissatisfaction and marginalization of the vast majority of developing countries notwithstanding, the GATT continued to exist for over four decades. In part, this longevity, especially remarkable given the difficult history of its unborn predecessor, derived from its ability to suit the needs of the major traders of the Western world. It covered the commercial interests of the developed countries, without making any intrusions into their domestic jurisdictions. Its weak institutional structure in terms of negotiation processes, decision-making procedures, and dispute settlement mechanism meant that developed countries would not resent its gentle bindings. In other words, the weaknesses of the GATT were critical in ensuring the commitment and participation of the major traders – the US, the European Community, Canada, and Japan (also known as the Quad group) – and thereby producing a far more meaningful treaty than an ITO without the US would have been.

The first four rounds of GATT negotiations dealt primarily with tariffs on goods. The weak institutional procedures of the GATT also allowed it sufficient flexibility to innovate and adapt to at least some international changes. Beginning in the Kennedy Round (1964–67), and more extensively in the Tokyo Round (1973–79), the GATT introduced a system of plurilateral codes (that is, codes signed on a voluntary basis by some countries rather than all the contracting parties) on issues that addressed newer forms of

1. Trade rounds in the GATT

Year	Place and name of round	Subjects covered	Number of par-ticipating countries
1947	Geneva	Tariffs	23
1949	Annecy	Tariffs	13
1951	Torquay	Tariffs	38
1956	Geneva	Tariffs	26
1960–1961	Geneva – Dillon Round	Tariffs	26
1964–1967	Geneva – Kennedy Round	Tariffs and anti-dumping measures	62
1973–1979	Geneva – Tokyo Round	Tariffs, non-tariff measures, 'frame-work' agreements	102
1986–1994	Geneva – Uruguay Round	Tariffs, non-tariff measures, rules, services, intellectual property, dispute settlement, textiles, agriculture, creation of the WTO, etc.	123

Source: Understanding the WTO, 3rd edition, August 2003 (WTO, Geneva)

protectionism. Its rules were extended to include sanitary and phytosanitary barriers to trade, technical barriers to trade, and other forms of Non-Tariff Barriers. The accession of developing countries also recorded a jump in this period. The GATT was growing in its mandate and size. In response to the changing comparative advantage of the developed countries, the Uruguay Round (1986–94) brought the so-called new issues within the mandate of the GATT: services, Trade-Related Intellectual Property

Rights, and Trade Related Investment Measures. In return for agreeing to these inclusions, developing countries were promised concessions on agriculture, textiles, and industrial goods.

The temporary arrangement of the GATT had not only survived for 47 years, it had flourished. Admittedly, it was a far less ambitious project than the ITO, and its lack of organizational structure generated several problems, especially as far as developing countries were concerned. But the same weaknesses of the GATT also ensured its political viability. The limited mandate of the GATT meant that it was not ridden with the many contradictions and impossible political compromises that the ITO was, while countries showed a greater willingness to commit to a treaty than have their hands tightly bound by a much more intrusive organization with a powerful dispute settlement mechanism. Developing countries, despite their frequent complaints about the exclusionary GATT system, were falling over each other to accede to the organization. Here was a model for a multilateral trade regime – if not an organization – that seemed to be working. Yet, in 1995, the old GATT was replaced with a new organization: the World Trade Organization.

Chapter 2
The creation of the World Trade Organization

The formation of the World Trade Organization in 1995 was a momentous event, particularly when held up against the history of unsuccessful attempts to establish such an organization. In this chapter, I analyse the political processes that led to the replacement of the General Agreement on Tariffs and Trade (GATT) with this new organization, and highlight the continuities and differences between the WTO and its predecessor.

Explaining the formation of the WTO

The creation of an international trade organization was a dream that had evaded trade negotiators of the post-war era for almost 50 years. The GATT was considered a poor substitute to the aborted International Trade Organization (ITO). But the attempts to form a multilateral trade organization continued. Some contracting parties of the GATT proposed the formation of a more permanent body, in the form of the Organization for Trade Cooperation, in 1955. But this proposal was no more successful than the ITO had been. The proposal for an international trade organization under UN auspices that was put forth in the Economic and Social Council (ECOSOC) in 1963 also came to naught. But when the Marrakesh Agreement concluded the Uruguay Round of Multilateral Trade Negotiations in 1994, the long-sought multilateral trade organization was born. Legally, the WTO came into existence on 1 January 1995, with a membership of 128 countries.

The emergence of the WTO in 1995 was partly a response to the changing imperatives of the international trading system in the 1980s. But its creation was also a function of the elaborate negotiation processes that resulted in what Sylvia Ostry has described as a 'Grand Bargain'. Without the processes of careful compromise and trade-offs, the WTO might have suffered the same fate as the ITO. In this section, we will rely on both sets of explanation – changing imperatives and negotiation processes – to analyse the formation of the WTO. One caveat, however, is worth bearing in mind. The negotiation processes and the resulting Grand Bargain were related very closely to the GATT, even though the WTO, as an international organization, may superficially resemble the ITO project. Subsequent chapters in this book illustrate that the persistence of GATT practices in the everyday workings of the WTO has had a critical influence on its nature and evolution as an international organization.

The creation of a multilateral trade organization was not on the agenda when the Uruguay Round was launched. But dissatisfaction with the GATT had been brewing in different quarters. Non-tariff barriers had proliferated in the 1970s. The Tokyo Round's invention of dealing with such barriers through voluntary codes was proving to be largely ineffective. The changing comparative advantage of developed countries, led by the US, demanded that the GATT would have to expand into the new issues of services, intellectual property rights, and investment measures if it wanted to keep the major traders aboard. Developing countries were also faced with new imperatives. The economic downturn of the 1980s led many of them to consider the East Asian model of export-oriented growth, and attempt to counter their widening deficits through an expansion of world trade. To implement such a growth strategy, to reap the benefits of unilateral liberalization, to protect themselves against increasing non-tariff barriers, and to ensure that the new issues were included in a manner and with a trade-off that supported their interests, developing countries had to go to the negotiating table. In response to this rising and active membership with new demands, it was inevitable that the agenda of the GATT was going to expand well beyond the traditional issue-areas of tariffs on goods. The Uruguay Round certainly saw such an expansion, and the old GATT structure was inadequate to deal with it.

One of the central problems facing negotiators in the Uruguay Round was to provide some coherence and integration to the multiple agreements that had emerged by the end of the Tokyo Round. International trade lawyer John Jackson pointed out that some of these codes were inconsistent with each other, and were enforced by different dispute settlement agreements with different memberships. It was recognized that unless a mechanism for coordinating this unwieldy set of agreements was found, the new agreements that were being negotiated in the Uruguay Round would make the system unsustainable. As a solution to this problem, Jackson proposed the creation of a world trade organization.

Coherence was not only a problem internal to the GATT, but also appeared in its dealings with the liberalization programmes that were managed by the World Bank and the IMF. A mechanism was needed to facilitate greater coordination between the GATT, the World Bank, and the IMF for the coherence of the international economic system. A trade organization, which might be able to maintain such external relations with other international organizations, emerged as the solution.

Once the idea of a world trade organization had been voiced, some contracting parties in the GATT began to see its advantages. Canada emerged as an active supporter, as did the EU. John Croome has traced the negotiating history of the Uruguay Round, and points out that the first formal paper for the establishment of such an organization came from the EU in June 1990. Besides meeting the need for greater coherence among the GATT codes, the EU proposal argued that a single dispute settlement system within the auspices of such an organization would be particularly advantageous. It also proposed that the limited nature of the GATT prevented it from taking on important functions such as trade policy reviews of the contracting parties and external negotiations with international organizations. The EU and Canada subsequently produced several detailed proposals together for the creation and running of a multilateral trade organization. But many countries still had to be convinced about the idea.

The suspicion of developing countries towards the idea of a multilateral trade organization was countered by incorporating the creation of the WTO into the Grand Bargain. In return for the inclusion of the 'new issues', the Single Undertaking, and the new organization of the WTO with its strengthened dispute settlement mechanism, developing countries were granted the inclusion of agriculture and textiles, and also special and differential treatment through longer time periods for implementing some of the new agreements. Once the Single Undertaking was extended to cover the Agreement establishing the WTO, the only choice that developing countries had was between agreeing to the entire package, including its potential costs, or surrendering all the new opportunities that the Uruguay Round agreements had opened up. They accepted the whole package and became members of the organization.

The US resistance to the organization under discussion was the longest-lasting. Gilbert Winham, drawing on the account by Deputy Director-General Warrant Lavorel, identifies the trade-off in which the US finally gave up its opposition in 1993. The US Chief Negotiator is reported to have said that the administration would be willing to rethink its opposition if all the other problems in the Round could be solved so that the administration would not risk opposition in the Congress by specific constituencies. The US finally dropped its opposition in return for an EU concession on computer chips and a change in the name of the organization from a Multilateral Trade Organization to the World Trade Organization.

3. The Final Act, marking the completion of the Uruguay Round, was signed in April 1994, at Marrakesh, Morocco. This comprehensive trade agreement covered 29 agreements that included the 'new issues' of services, intellectual property rights, and investment measures, and an additional 36,000 pages of national schedules on goods and services.

The creation of the WTO was certainly a response to problems with which the old GATT structure could no longer cope. But its creation was equally a result of the conscious exclusion of certain controversial areas and weak agreements in others. The Agreement on Agriculture was an important step in bringing agriculture into the fold of some general rules. But as Chapter 4 shows, the Agreement left vast scope for continued protectionism to meet the requirements of the major trading nations. The General Agreement on Trade in Services included Mode 4, that is, trade in services through the movement of people, but actual commitments on this mode were few. Unlike the ITO, and in continuation with GATT practices, the WTO coverage did not extend to labour standards, commodity agreements, or monopolistic business practices. The next chapter demonstrates that despite attempts to formalize and legalize some of the decision-making procedures, the WTO adhered to GATT practices. These exclusions and weaknesses have, in several instances, created inconsistencies within the WTO, which will also be discussed later in the book. But at least at the time of its creation, these limitations ensured the support of the major trading nations. The foundations of the WTO rested firmly on its limited ambition.

4. The Centre William Rappard – the building that had housed the GATT Secretariat since 1977 – continues to serve as the home for the WTO. It was the first building erected specifically to house an international organization. Prior to moving into the Centre William Rappard, the GATT Secretariat was housed in the Villas Bocage and Fenêtre, located in close proximity to the Palais des Nations, the UN headquarters in Geneva.

Principles underlying the WTO

Two key principles underlie the agreements of the WTO. Both are GATT-derived and point to the continuities between the WTO and its predecessor.

The idea of non-discrimination holds the key to multilateralism in the GATT and the WTO. In their seminal work on the WTO, Bernard Hoekman and Michel Kostecki identify two components to the principle of non-discrimination: the Most Favoured Nation (MFN) rule and national treatment. The MFN rule in the WTO derives from Article 1 in the GATT. Paraphrased by Hoekman and Kostecki, the rule 'requires that a product made in one member country be treated no less favourably than a like good that originates in any other country'. In other words, a concession granted by any one party to another in the WTO must be multilateralized to all other parties. The MFN rule applies to all issues included within the mandate of the WTO. The exceptions allowed are few and clearly specified. They extend to regional trade agreements, preferential treatment for developing countries, and the invocation of a non-application clause by an existing member against a newly acceding country.

The second aspect of the principle of non-discrimination – national treatment – requires member countries to treat foreign goods no less favourably than domestically produced like goods, once the former have met whatever border measures are applied by the particular country. The national treatment rule is derived from Part II of the original GATT. However, as explained in Chapter 1, the Protocol of Provisional Application had allowed countries to circumvent national treatment by claiming grandfathering rights. This has changed with the creation of the WTO, in which national treatment is a general obligation in all issue areas, with the sole exception of trade in services.

The second principle underlying all WTO agreements is reciprocity, which also guided all tariff reductions under the GATT. Reciprocity is an important mechanism that limits free riding (that might otherwise become rampant on the strength of the non-discrimination principle). It also makes the process of agreeing to tariff concessions politically palatable at home. This same principle of reciprocity, however, has been a sore point in the relations of developed and developing countries in both the GATT and the WTO. The Indian delegate is widely cited as having declaimed in the early years of the GATT: 'Equality of treatment is equitable only among equals. A weakling cannot carry the burden of a giant.' The principle of non-reciprocity for developing countries was begrudgingly accepted in the GATT in the Tokyo Round through the 'Enabling Clause'. This provision created a legal basis in the GATT for the Generalized System of Preferences – a system of special and differential treatment (S&D) – that had been established under the auspices of the United Nations Conference on Trade and Development. But this provision itself ironically came with a *quid pro quo* by the inclusion of the graduation principle, which requires developing countries to return to the game of multilateral reciprocity once they have moved up the development ladder. In the WTO, the provisions of S&D have been further diluted and largely limited to longer time periods for implementation of the agreements and technical assistance to facilitate this.

In addition to these two broad principles, the WTO resembles the GATT through its reliance on transparency, enforceability of the commitments, and the existence of 'safety valves' that allow governments to restrict trade under certain circumstances. In fact, the formation of the WTO has enhanced the transparency requirement and enforceability provisions of the agreements. Not only are members required to publish their trade regulations and notify changes, but their policies are subject to surveillance by the Secretariat through the Trade Policy Review Mechanism. Should a country renege on its commitments, the stronger dispute settlement of the WTO can authorize punitive measures. These features are discussed in greater detail in Chapter 5.

So how is the WTO different from the GATT?

The preceding sections have illustrated the continuities between the GATT and the WTO. The latter continues to function as a forum for negotiations and provides a code of conduct as the GATT had done. These continuities, however, beg the question why the WTO has attracted so much more popular angst and apprehension than its predecessor ever did. The answer lies in the legal nature of the WTO, which makes it quite a different animal from the GATT. Despite their many similarities, the two differ markedly in six important ways.

First, the GATT was legally no more than a multilateral treaty among contracting parties; the WTO is an international organization with a membership. Article I of the Agreement establishing the WTO explicitly refers to the establishment of an *organization*. The WTO is entrusted with the task of providing 'the common institutional framework for the conduct of trade relations among its Members' (Article II). The Agreement specifies an elaborate organizational structure that is to underlie the functioning of the WTO and further enables the organization to cooperate with other international organizations that have responsibilities related to the WTO's. The WTO enjoys a legal personality that the GATT could not.

Second, as the last chapter explained, the GATT was applied only on a provisional basis; the Protocol of Provisional Application ('Grandfather Clause') exempted contracting parties from applying some important GATT articles if they were inconsistent with existent legislation. The WTO, in contrast, was created as an organization in its own right rather than as a provisional measure. As a result, even though the US managed to preserve one grandfather right, the general principle of grandfather rights no

5. The adoption of the official logo of the WTO was described by the then Director-General, Mr Renato Ruggiero, as 'another step in establishing this unique institution on a firm and lasting foundation'

longer exists. This means that member countries can no longer appeal to pre-existing domestic legislation to avoid adherence to the agreements of the WTO. They will have to do whatever it takes, even if this involves amending domestic laws, to abide by the rules of the WTO or risk retaliation.

The third feature of the WTO that distinguishes it from the GATT is that all its agreements (including the Dispute Settlement Understanding, besides the substantive agreements on goods, services, investment measures, and intellectual property rights) are held together by the Single Undertaking. The Single Undertaking means that participating countries cannot selectively apply the range of agreements that exist within the WTO. The Single Undertaking approach presents the polar opposite of the approach that the GATT had evolved by the time of the Tokyo Round. By the end of the 1970s, the GATT had come to include several plurilateral agreements that countries could pick and choose to abide by. The resulting large cluster of over 180 agreements often produced differing purposes, differing memberships, and included agreements that were sometimes inconsistent with the GATT. The Single Undertaking sought to get rid of these legal inconsistencies and complexities. Given the range of issues covered in the Uruguay Round, the Single Undertaking was also a device to catalyse trade-offs among negotiating countries across issues, and thereby facilitate an overall multilateral agreement that met the top priorities of most parties. When the Uruguay Round was completed, the Single Undertaking concept was developed to mean that all the signatories to the Marrakesh Agreement would have to become members of the WTO. The WTO, and all the agreements within its umbrella, came as a single package, which countries would have to accept on an all-or-nothing basis.

Fourth, the mandate of the WTO was significantly more intrusive than that of GATT. The GATT's foray into rules on non-tariff barriers (NTBs) had been only through the mechanism of the plurilateral codes. This changed in the WTO through the Single Undertaking. But further, the Uruguay Round expanded the reach of the agreements to issues that went well beyond border measures. The WTO covers not only the traditional area of trade in goods, as per the GATT, but also has agreements on services, trade-related intellectual property rights (TRIPs), and trade-related investment measures (TRIMs). Even in the case of trade in goods, the WTO now extends its regulation to issues such as sanitary and phytosanitary barriers to trade (SPS) and technical barriers to trade (TBT).

Fifth, again in response to the problems that arose from having several different dispute resolution arrangements that matched with the particular plurilateral code of the Tokyo Round, the WTO has a significantly stronger Dispute Settlement Mechanism (DSM). A detailed discussion of the DSM appears in Chapter 5. Suffice it to note at this point that the WTO's DSM enjoys the rule of 'negative consensus'. This means that to overturn the findings of a panel, there has to be a consensus on the overrule (as opposed to the GATT practice, where consensus was required for the adoption of a panel ruling, which gave the losing party the right to block). Further, the Single Undertaking allows cross-issue retaliation under the DSM, so countries can punish violators of agreements where it hurts them most.

Finally, given the new organizational stature of the WTO, the Secretariat has now been formally constituted to replace the Interim Commission for the International Trade Organization (ICITO) of the GATT. It is true that the WTO Secretariat, to this day, remains minuscule in comparison to those of the IMF and the World Bank. But its powers have been considerably expanded since GATT days, including greater surveillance functions through the Trade Policy Review Mechanism (to be discussed in Chapter 5).

Given all the above features, members of the WTO are far more deeply bound to its rules than the contracting parties of the GATT ever were. These rules are more intrusive than those negotiated in the GATT; they are more formalized; and they enjoy increased enforceability through the enhanced DSM that the previous regime could not afford. The organizational structure of the WTO provides an excellent illustration of how the WTO builds on some old GATT features but formalizes and legalizes them in a way so unprecedented that the resulting change is a qualitative one.

Organizational structure

Article IV of the Agreement establishing the WTO specifies its organizational structure. An overview of the structures provides us with the first cut towards an understanding of how democratic, egalitarian, or efficient the WTO is as an international organization.

6. In May 1995, Renato Ruggiero took over from Peter Sutherland as the new Director-General of the WTO

Perhaps the most important feature of the structure of the WTO is that it is a member-driven organization. It stands here in striking contrast to the IMF and the World Bank, which have been described as staff-driven organizations, where governments work in close conjunction with the staff and the Executive Board. In the WTO, the onus of negotiating the agreements, implementing them, and enforcing them falls on the members themselves. This member-driven character of the WTO derives directly from the GATT, whose lack of organizational status placed all responsibilities for conducting any treaty-related business on the signatories themselves. Delegation of powers to a secretariat or an executive board was impossible under the circumstances. The WTO has continued this practice. If there is any international organization whose structure ensures that it is made of its members, for its members, and by its members, the WTO is it.

The flip side of this coin is the small size of the WTO Secretariat and its limited functions of providing technical and administrative support for the members. The Secretariat has been formally constituted in the WTO on a permanent basis, and thereby presents a departure from the temporary secretariat of the GATT. Some of its powers have been expanded in its role of providing technical assistance and conducting Trade Policy Reviews. But in most other matters, the nature of the WTO Secretariat is not very different from the GATT's. In comparison to other international organizations, the WTO Secretariat continues to be small; at the time of writing, it comprised only about 600 members of staff (in contrast to the well over 6,000-strong World Bank). Unlike the Fund and the Bank, which generate their own income, the WTO budget is small and comes from the contributions of members. These contributions are assessed according to the trade shares of the member countries. Countries may, in addition to their contribution, voluntarily provide funds directed towards specific purposes, such as the provision of technical assistance and capacity-building by the Secretariat.

The Secretariat is headed by the director-general, whose 'powers, duties, conditions of service and term of office' are all determined by the members in the form of the Ministerial Conference. In practice, however, this is a powerful position, and director-generals in the past have played a central role in the negotiation process as agenda-setters and mediators. Countries have therefore vied hard to place their favoured candidate into this choice position, and the selection process has been a fraught one. Animosities came to the fore in the lead-up to the Seattle Ministerial Conference in 1999, when the term of Renato Ruggiero, the first director-general of the WTO, was coming to an end. Precious time that should have been spent over the agenda for the Seattle Ministerial was instead lost in the leadership struggle, and is seen by many as having contributed to the failure of the Seattle Ministerial Conference. A compromise was finally arrived at, and it was agreed that the term of the director-general would be shared between the two candidates, with Mike Moore of New Zealand succeeding Ruggiero for three years, and Supachai Panitchpakdi of Thailand taking over for the next three years. Learning from bitter experience, negotiators came up with a set of guidelines to assist in subsequent selection processes and mitigate potential conflict, even though most recognize that it will be impossible to sanitize the process from realpolitik.

The Ministerial Conference constitutes the topmost decision-making body in the WTO, thereby reinforcing its member-driven character. It is made up of the ministers responsible for trade affairs for all its member countries. The Ministerial Conference has a long-established tradition in the GATT. But in the GATT, these conferences were held infrequently, usually at the time of the launch of a new round of multilateral trade negotiations. The WTO institutionalized the Ministerial Conference through Article IV.1 of the Agreement: 'There shall be a Ministerial Conference composed of representatives of all the Members, which shall meet at least once every two years.' While this practice ensures a political commitment and institutional continuity for the WTO that the GATT never enjoyed, it has also come under criticism. Many developing countries complain that the frequency of ministerial meetings imparts a pace to WTO negotiations that they cannot keep up with.

The everyday functioning of the WTO is managed through an elaborate structure that is based in Geneva and is also composed of its members, illustrated in Figure 7. Except for about 22 countries, all the other members of the WTO send delegations to their permanent missions in Geneva to enable participation in the WTO. The topmost Geneva-based WTO body is the General Council, which carries out the functions assigned to it by the agreements and by the Ministerial Conference. The General Council meets regularly at the WTO headquarters in Geneva and is open to all the delegates. It also meets in the guise of the Trade Policy Review Body and Dispute Settlement Body.

Below the General Council are three sector-specific councils: the Council for Trade in Goods, the Council for Trade in Services, and the Council for Trade-Related Intellectual Property Rights. At the same level as these three councils are five committees that deal with more specific issues. Their coverage extends to trade and environment; trade and development (with a sub-committee on Least Developed Countries); regional trade agreements; balance of payments restrictions; and budget, finance, and administration. In addition to these, there are working parties dealing with accessions, and working groups that carry out exploratory work in the areas of trade and investment, competition policy, and transparency in government procurement. The three councils, and the independent committees, working parties, and working groups, report back to the General Council. Plurilateral committees, dealing with a small group of agreements signed only by a part of the membership, also form part of the GATT structure. At the time of a multilateral negotiation, new committees can be created to facilitate the negotiation process. In 2001, for instance, at the Doha Ministerial Conference, a new Trade Negotiations Committee was created to negotiate the Doha Development Agenda (discussed in Chapter 6).

At the next level are committees that deal with specific issues in goods and services, and thus exist within the auspices of the sectoral

WTO structure

All WTO members may participate in all councils, committees, etc, except Appellate Body, Dispute Settlement panels, and plurilateral committees.

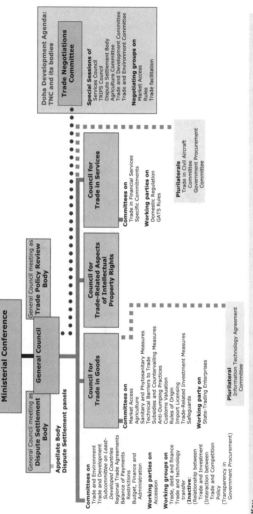

Key

- ▬ Reporting to General Council (or a subsidiary)
- ▬ Reporting to Dispute Settlement Body
- ▬ Plurilateral committees inform the General Council or Goods Council of their activities, although these agreements are not signed by all WTO members
- •••• Trade Negotiations Committee reports to General Council

The General Council also meets as the Trade Policy Review Body and Dispute Settlement Body

7. **The organizational structure of the WTO**

committees on Trade in Goods and Trade in Services. All these meetings are open to the entire membership of the WTO. The exceptions are the committees on the plurilateral agreements, the Textiles Monitoring Body, and the dispute settlement panels and Appellate Body.

All the councils, committees, working groups, and working parties meet according to the Members' agenda at the time and their requirements. But the expansiveness of the WTO agenda, and the resulting proliferation of appropriate organizational structures, is reflected in the very large number of meetings that are called in the WTO. In addition to these formal meetings, WTO diplomacy thrives on informal meetings at different levels (discussed in detail in the next chapter). Hoekman and Kostecki, writing in 2001, estimated that all these formal and informal meetings added up to about 1,200 meetings a year. With the launch of a new round of Multilateral Trade Negotiations as per the Doha Development Agenda of November 2001, the number of these meetings has increased further.

All the organizational structures of the WTO are constituted by member governments and their representatives. Non-governmental organizations (NGOs) or interest groups have no direct entry into the WTO. Article V.2 of the Agreement establishing the WTO states only that: 'The General Council may make appropriate arrangements for consultation and cooperation with non-governmental organizations concerned with matters related to those of the WTO.' Particularly in the aftermath of the debacle at the Seattle Ministerial Conference in 1999, where the legitimacy of the WTO came under serious challenge as a result of mass demonstrations by NGOs of various descriptions, the WTO has made some attempt to engage with non-governmental actors. NGOs can go through a process of accreditation and gain access to some meetings in the Ministerial Conferences. The Appellate Body has also begun to allow *amicus curiae* briefs (literally, 'friend of the court') from NGOs (to be discussed in

Chapter 5). But even here, the WTO website provides the following interpretation:

> When the Appellate Body receives unsolicited briefs directly from an *amicus curiae*, the entity filing the brief has no right to have it considered. Nonetheless, the Appellate Body maintains that it has authority to accept and consider any information it considers pertinent and useful in deciding an appeal, including unsolicited *amicus curiae* submissions.

All in all, if a particular interest group wishes to influence WTO rules, it can do so only through its government. Of course, WTO officials and negotiators recognize that their decisions affect domestic constituencies within countries. But given the member-driven character of the organization, the onus of dealing with the distributive consequences of WTO regulations falls on the member governments rather than the WTO as an international organization.

An analysis of the structures of the WTO reveals an interesting paradox. In many ways, the WTO is one of the most expansive and intrusive organizations of its time. Its Ministerial Conference and many committees make rules that go deep inside the borders of states. Members must adhere to these rules or face retaliation. But simultaneously, the legacy of the GATT has ensured that the WTO is also a very weak organization in other ways. The organization, up to its highest decision-making body – the Ministerial Conference – is made up of the members themselves. The members have not had to surrender any of their decision-making powers to a secretariat, or delegate them to an executive body. Any rules that the members must implement are ones that they themselves made in the councils and committees (which are open to all of them). Any punitive action has to be exercised by the member rather the collective body, and even the Dispute Settlement Body that authorizes such retaliations is ultimately the same as the General Council and therefore constituted by country delegates. Given this rather frail existence of the WTO as an international organization, one might well wonder why the WTO has attracted charges of a democratic deficit. The answer can be found, not in the seemingly democratic structures of the WTO, but in the processes of negotiation and decision-making that underlie them.

Chapter 3
Decision-making and negotiation processes

The WTO, as an international organization, is characterized by a legalism that had evaded the GATT because of its provisional nature. But as we shall find in this chapter, alongside the powerful legalism of its agreements, structures, and enforcement capacity sit informal and *ad hoc* GATT-derived decision-making and negotiation processes. These processes may have worked for the GATT, whose legal standing, mandate, and active membership were limited, and which could (just about) function as an exclusive club. But the use of those same processes by the significantly more powerful WTO is highly problematic. At the heart of the WTO lies a major and unsustainable discrepancy: extreme legalization, particularly in the enforcement of its rules through the dispute settlement mechanism, on the one hand, and an inordinate reliance on *de facto* improvisation in the making of those rules, on the other. This incongruity is important in terms of the coherence (or the lack thereof) of the WTO as an international institution. But it also has some far-reaching implications for the existing power asymmetries within the WTO.

In this chapter, I will explore the principal features of these processes, and illustrate ways in which rules and procedures make a difference. My central argument here is that the standard operating procedures of the WTO are a reflection of power imbalances between the developed and developing countries, and they further exacerbate these inequalities. The first part of the chapter focuses on decision-making processes in the WTO, while the second highlights its negotiation rules and formulae.

Decision-making processes in the WTO

In terms of its everyday workings, the WTO codifies many of the processes that had evolved in the GATT regime. Three features are central to all its decision-making processes: voting rules, the norm of consensus-based decision-making, and the importance of informal procedures that underlie all the stated formalities.

Voting procedures

First, and deriving directly from GATT practice, the WTO is a one-member-one-vote organization, in striking contrast to the IMF and the World Bank which have systems of weighted voting. For instance, in the case of the IMF, the voting power of countries depends on the size of their respective quotas, which in turn are supposed to reflect their weights in the international economy. The Agreement establishing the WTO, however, explicitly states that each member shall have one vote in meetings, and further ensures that formal meetings, barring a few exceptions that were highlighted in the previous chapter, shall be open to the entire membership.

In terms of the actual counting of votes, most important decisions in the WTO are supposed to be taken by means of a simple majority. Exceptions to this rule are specified in Articles IX and X of the Agreement and in the relevant plurilateral agreement. In this matter too, the WTO presents a contrast to the IMF and the World Bank, where most decisions require an 85% majority. This gives effective veto power to the US, which commands about 17.5% of the votes. The requirement of a simple majority for a decision to be accepted in the WTO is important in that it imparts considerable voting power to developing countries, which form well over two-thirds of the entire membership. Interestingly, however, developing countries have never actually sought recourse to their overwhelming strength in numbers, in contrast to the UN General Assembly, which has often been ridden with the tyranny of the majority. The reason for this can be found in the second tenet of WTO decision-making: the norm of consensus.

Decision-making on the basis of consensus

Despite the existence of elaborate voting procedures, most decisions in the GATT were in practice taken on the basis of consensus. This GATT practice has been codified in Article IX.1 of the Agreement establishing the WTO. Consensus is arrived at 'if no Member, present at the meeting when the decision is taken, formally objects to the proposed decision'. The most immediate power implication of this practice is that developing countries have never been able to make use of the power of large numbers in the GATT or the WTO. But consensus-based decision-making disadvantages developing countries in several other ways.

8. Consensus-based decision-making at work!

First, the simple requirement of the consensus norm, that no member *present* objects to the decision, translates into quite a difficult condition for developing countries. About 22 member countries of the WTO have no delegations present in Geneva to voice their objection to the decision under discussion. Even for those countries with a presence in Geneva, attendance is an issue when several parallel meetings are involved. In a study that this author conducted in 2001, the average size of a developing country delegation was less than half the average size of a developed country delegation. Even a presence in all the multiple meetings in the WTO is difficult under these circumstances, let alone an informed and active presence. Especially in the context of the member-driven character of the WTO (discussed in the previous chapter), where the onus of preparation and participation for a WTO meeting falls on the members themselves, developing countries find themselves ill-equipped to participate effectively in the consensus-making process. Second, deriving again from the GATT, exclusive, club-like meetings are often used for the purpose of reaching consensus. As the majority developing countries have traditionally found themselves frequently excluded from such meetings, consensus-based decision making is interpreted by at least some countries as an exclusionary device that the strong use against the weak. Small-group meetings in the WTO, however, are not simply a product of the consensus norm. Rather, they form part of the third feature of WTO decision-making: a general culture, again GATT-derived, which has thrived on informal diplomatic procedures rather than formal rules of negotiation.

The importance of informal processes in WTO diplomacy

The importance of informal processes in the WTO derives at least partly from the GATT's use of the so-called Principal Supplier Principle (PSP), which usually involved initial discussions between the principal supplier and consumer rather than an open discussion involving the entire membership. It is also a product of the equal representation that it allows its members, which means that several other processes are needed besides the plenary meetings to beat the consensus into shape. The importance of informal processes in trade diplomacy is recognized even on the WTO website. Some informal consultations, such as the Heads of Delegations meetings (HODs), can involve the entire membership. Others involve smaller groups, such as the so-called Green Room meetings that take place at the initiative of the director-general. The existence of these informal processes allows members to exercise the flexibility that is often key to brokering compromise in a difficult trade negotiation. But when informality and a lack of rules become effectively written into the very basis of an institution, two sets of problems emerge.

The first set of problems is a lack of transparency and predictability. For developing countries, which attach considerable value to the predictability that comes from belonging to a rules-based institution, informality generates some serious difficulties. Green Room meetings in the GATT, and the WTO, were until recently especially notorious for this: the old-style Green Room worked by invitation only, and even the list of invitees was treated as confidential. Particularly in the aftermath of the failed Seattle Ministerial Conference, the opaqueness of such consultations and their exclusionary effects came under severe criticism. For instance, before the Seattle talks were brought to a close, African trade ministers issued the following statement on 2 December 1999:

> There is no transparency in the proceedings and African countries are being marginalised and generally excluded on issues of vital importance for our peoples and their future. We are particularly concerned over the stated intentions to produce a ministerial text at any cost including at the cost of procedures designed to secure participation and consensus.

> We reject the approach that is being employed and we must point out that under the present circumstances, we will not be able to join the consensus required to meet the objectives of the Ministerial Conference.

A group of Latin American and Caribbean countries issued a similar statement. In the face of such trenchant criticism, a conscious attempt has been made by all parties concerned to improve the process. The schedules of small-group meetings and the list of invitees are now announced; members can self-select participation; at least some minutes are published; and the meetings are open-ended and directed only towards consensus-building rather than any decision-making. But several problems persist. Often developing countries find that they are not well-equipped to even identify their interests in some of the highly technical areas to claim their right to participation in a small-group meeting. They also find that they are unable to exercise the threat to block in the final stages of decision-making if they have not attended the consensus-building small-group meetings. In addition to this, informality places considerable discretion in the hands of the chairpersons at all levels of the WTO hierarchy. These key individuals define the agenda and frequency of meetings as well as the lists of invitees, and can thereby exercise an important influence on negotiated outcomes. In the absence of rules about exactly what the chair can do and how he or she can do it, the role that certain chairpersons choose to play inevitably becomes a source of conflict. Finally, the importance of informal processes means that the WTO retains what Rubens Ricupero, Secretary General of the United Nations Conference on Trade and Development (UNCTAD), describes as the 'almost English club atmosphere' of the GATT. This inaccessible culture of the institution, along with language barriers, makes effective participation an especially daunting task for the smaller and newer members of the WTO. As a result, developing countries, in coalitions or individually, have put forth proposals for institutional reform that envisage a WTO whose functioning is tightly bound by a clearly specified set of formal rules and procedures.

The second set of problems resulting from the lack of specific rules to govern the WTO is that it makes the WTO especially prone to power-based improvisation. In the absence of generally agreed rules to deal with difficult situations, we have examples of several stop-gap measures that are somehow cobbled together to become a part of the customary practice of the WTO. Decisions arrived at on the basis of such contested rules are bound to lack legitimacy. Examples of problems deriving from such haphazard improvisation and *ad hoc* rule-making abound in the short history of the WTO. The last Ministerial Conference that was held in Cancun in September 2003 provides some useful examples of these problems. The outcome of the Cancun Ministerial process is discussed in detail in Chapter 6. At this point, suffice it to note that conference ended in deadlock., which was at least as much a product of some questionable negotiation and decision-making processes gone seriously awry, as substantive disagreements among the negotiating parties.

All WTO Ministerial Conferences use a draft text of some kind as the starting point for the negotiation. The traditional GATT and WTO practice for drafting a text for a Ministerial Conference involved putting together a 'bracketed text', that is, a text in which all the contested proposals of different parties were put within square brackets and were negotiated at the ministerial conference. But in the run-up to the Cancun Ministerial, the Chair of the General Council, Ambassador Carlos Perez del Castillo, issued a draft text for the Ministerial 'on his own responsibility' in close cooperation with the Director-General. The Castillo draft did 'not purport to be agreed in any part on this stage', and claimed to be without prejudice to any delegation's position on any issue. Nonetheless, the text played a critical role in setting the agenda for negotiation at the Cancun Ministerial, particularly in the parts that it chose to include and exclude. For instance, it was seen to favour the position of some developed countries through its inclusion of modalities for negotiating the 'Singapore issues' (so-called after the Singapore Ministerial of 1996, where some developed countries had tried to expand WTO coverage to trade and investment, competition policy, government procurement, and trade facilitation). Since 1996, developing countries had consistently fought tooth and nail against even an inclusion of these issues, let alone agree upon the modalities for their negotiations. The reaction of developing countries to this text was, expectedly, hostile. They attacked it not only for its substance, but also for constituting the chair's text rather than the traditional bracketed text. And yet the Castillo draft was used as the text for the Cancun Ministerial Conference.

The fact that the Castillo draft was issued in the first place and further utilized as the draft ministerial text in Cancun in spite of such opposition can be explained by the precedent that it had in the Harbinson draft. Stuart Harbinson, as the Chair of the General Council, had issued a similar draft in the run-up to the Doha Ministerial Conference in 2001. Developing countries had questioned the authority of the chair to issue such a text; some had lambasted the draft for ignoring their viewpoints. Nonetheless, the text was used as the draft ministerial text for the Doha conference; it provided the precedent for the Castillo draft at Cancun; and in the absence of any rules on the process of arriving at a text or defining the role of the chair, developing countries could do little of consequence to stop this process. The episode illustrates how, in the absence of clear rules about decision-making in the WTO, the powerful are able to improvise precedents to their advantage. Attempts by the weak to overturn such precedents are usually unsuccessful.

Another example of such controversial rule improvisation can be found in the notion of 'explicit consensus'. As a result of India's insistence at the Doha Ministerial Conference, the final text agreed that negotiations on the Singapore issues would take place in the fifth ministerial conference, the Cancun Ministerial, 'on the basis of a decision to be taken, by explicit consensus, at that session'. The insertion of this phrase was regarded as a major victory for developing countries. In practice, however, the phrase had no legal foundation or precise definition, and it left room for the inevitable dispute that followed at Cancun. Developing countries' interpretation of the phrase was that explicit consensus was necessary for any negotiation on the Singapore issues; developed countries saw it as implying there already existed agreement on starting the negotiations and explicit consensus was needed only on modalities. Much of this conflict at Cancun could have been avoided had there been adequate definitions and rules in place.

Cancun also saw complaints by developing countries about the process of appointment of the so-called 'Facilitators' and also the way in which they carried out their appointed tasks. This practice of choosing Facilitators (also referred to as 'Friends of the Chair'), to assist the Chairperson of the Ministerial Conference in small-group consultations over specific issues, has some precedence in the GATT and the WTO. However, no attempt has been made to clarify the basis or criteria of this selection process; as a result, it has frequently been dogged by controversy. Recognizing the crucial role that Facilitators can play in agenda-setting, developing countries at Cancun questioned the process of selection, and their method of operation and resulting outcomes. Many felt that their persistent opposition to several paragraphs within the original text, particularly on agriculture and the Singapore issues, had been blatantly ignored until the final day of the conference as a result of such poor 'facilitating'.

Finally, the scale on which rules are missing in the WTO is illustrated in the controversy generated by the simple decision of drawing the conference proceedings to a close. All precedent had led members to believe that the Cancun meeting would continue well after the scheduled deadline of 14 September. The decision taken by Minister Derbez to close the conference as per the scheduled deadline generated vociferous and mixed reactions. Some alleged that Derbez had come under US pressure; others criticized him for his lack of appreciation of the shenanigans and brinkmanship that have come to characterize GATT/WTO meetings; still others praised him for managing to salvage the conference through the perfunctory six-paragraph declaration.

These debates, however, miss the important purpose of belonging to an organization such as the WTO, which is to provide its members with a credible set of rules and guidelines for their multilateral interaction. By adhering to old GATT habits, and its culture of corridor diplomacy and unwritten protocols of interaction, the WTO is unable to fulfil this crucial function.

Negotiation processes in the WTO

The substance and evolution of the agenda of the WTO depends to a large extent on the decision-making processes. Several of these decision-making procedures are themselves the product of negotiation. As we discovered in the previous section, protocols on the negotiation of such rules are few and often result in the reliance on *de facto*, controversial processes of rule formation. But especially after the agenda is set, formal and informal negotiation processes are crucial in determining what goes into the final package. Without such protocols of negotiation in place, the *raison d'être* for the WTO – to provide a negotiating forum that facilitates multilateral trade liberalization – would collapse. Of course, any negotiation is driven by the preferences of states, their domestic constituencies, and the individual negotiators party to the deal. But the fact that countries engage in tariff reductions within the WTO matters: the WTO establishes certain rules of the game, which would not automatically come into existence and in whose absence different outcomes would ensue. Below, I examine the principal features of the negotiation process, and also provide examples of how negotiation minutiae can sometimes skew outcomes in favour of the already powerful in the WTO.

First, as the previous chapter outlined, the WTO provides its members with two firm rules that provide the basis for all trade negotiations under its auspices: the Most Favoured Nation (MFN) rule and the associated principle of reciprocity. The first extends all concessions negotiated between two parties to the rest of the membership, thereby expanding the pie to be shared and also shielding countries against the vagaries of bilateralism. To guard against free-riding and make trade liberalization politically palatable at home, however, the second principle of reciprocity is crucial. Concessions negotiated under these rules have to be bound; if countries exceed the bound level, they can be penalized (barring specific circumstances when this is allowed). While these rules existed in the GATT, the WTO has strengthened them through its powerful dispute-settlement mechanism that authorizes retaliation if a party reneges on its obligations, and also by extending it to all countries including developing countries (to be discussed in detail in Chapter 4). It is worth bearing in mind that the two rules of MFN and reciprocity are actually mutually contradictory. The WTO resolves these contradictions by building in the condition of reciprocity to MFN in the negotiation process; once the concession has been granted, however, its multilateralization is essential and cannot subsequently be made conditional on reciprocity.

Second, the WTO has evolved specific methods of actually implementing the broader rules of MFN and reciprocity, with implications for the inclusion or exclusion of certain parties and certain agendas. For instance, in the first five rounds under GATT auspices, the Principal Supplier Principle was used in tariff negotiations. As per this principle, the initial negotiation would be conducted bilaterally among the largest countries on specific products. Hoekman and Kostecki explain the rationale behind this:

> Granting a concession to a small supplier implies giving away the concession to the principal supplier, since the latter will benefit from it due to the MFN rule. The principal supplier is the trading nation which benefits the most from a concession and is thus probably prepared to offer more reciprocal trade liberalization than a smaller supplier would be prepared or able to do.

Smaller countries may enter into the negotiation in the endgame, when the country granting a concession to the principal supplier might make the offer conditional on gaining supplementary concessions from other smaller suppliers of the same product. However, as discussed in Chapter 1, negotiations based on this principle resulted in the marginalization of developing countries and their agendas from the GATT process. Further, as the number of products on the GATT agenda and its membership expanded, negotiations on a product-by-product basis became unmanageably complex.

To address some of the problems of the Principal Supplier Principle, across-the-board tariff negotiations were used in the Kennedy Round. Two types of formulae were used for this: the linear cutting formula and the harmonizing formula. The former requires all members to engage in the same rate of tariff cuts for all product lines. It allows a broader coverage, but also means that countries with higher tariffs can continue to have high tariffs in relation to other members implementing the same rates of tariff cuts. The harmonization formula can have many versions; depending on the particular formula used, it can reduce higher tariffs much more drastically than lower ones. The choice of formula can be a difficult political matter, especially as the distributive implications of each type vary across and within countries. Exactly how politicized the process of choosing a negotiation formula can be was illustrated at the Cancun meeting, where one of the principal causes for the breakdown of the negotiations was that countries could not agree upon the formula that would provide the basis for the Doha agricultural negotiations. Even after an across-the-board formula was adopted in the Kennedy Round, a mix-and-match approach was used in the Kennedy and Tokyo Rounds in practice. The Uruguay Round saw the use of a sector-by-sector approach rather than a formula approach. Today, a mix of approaches is used depending on the issue area. For instance, after the agreement on the 'July Package' in the summer of 2004 (discussed in Chapter 6), a tiered formula is going to be used in agriculture, while services negotiations will continue to be on a request-offer basis among countries. Services commitments by countries have in general been disappointing so far; some observers attribute this to the request-offer approach and argue that it needs to be substituted with a more generalized approach.

Third, multilateral trade negotiations depend critically on issue linkage for their success. Country A agrees to make a concession on Issue I that is of value to Country B, but, in return, gains a concession from Country B on Issue II that is of particular value to Country A. In other words, issue linkage facilitates reciprocal exchange. This exchange also increases the potential gains from trade liberalization according to the respective preferences of negotiating countries. Without such linkages, multilateral trade liberalization would be a considerably more difficult process than it already is; indeed, the creation of the WTO would have been impossible without them. The practice of issue linkage is epitomized in the concept of the Single Undertaking.

While issue linkages can facilitate agreement, they also have a negative side, as they can be used by powerful countries to extract disproportionate concessions from their weaker counterparts. Frequently cited examples are of the Uruguay Round, when developing countries gained some concessions on agriculture and textiles, but paid a heavy price for those concessions through the inclusion of the 'new issues'. Linkages can also extend beyond the issue area of trade. Politicians from developed countries have been known to offer bilateral carrots and sticks to developing countries in return for their agreeing to withdraw from a certain position or to agree to a concession. Examples of such carrots include aid, low-interest loans, market access quotas, and regional trade arrangements, while threats of withdrawing these concessions and privileges are brandished as sticks.

Issue linkage can exacerbate power asymmetries, especially if they are used to make weak countries pay several times over for the same concession. The coalition of developing countries known as the Like Minded Group (LMG) was in effect making this same argument when it threatened to block the launch of the round of trade negotiations that is currently underway (the so-called 'Doha Development Agenda'). The LMG highlighted the many problems that developing countries have encountered in implementing the Uruguay Round. These implementation problems referred to the costs of implementation, as well as the fact that developed countries have not kept their end of the Uruguay Round bargain, and hence the fruits of the Uruguay Round have proven elusive for developing countries. They argued that if they agreed to a new round and gained the concession that the implementation issues would be put onto the agenda of the new round, they would end up paying again for the unrealized promises of the Uruguay Round through more concessions on new issue areas. It is on account of these kinds of negative issue linkages that the Single Undertaking has attracted considerable criticism in certain quarters.

Fourth, underlying all processes in any international organization is its organizational culture, which can have an important effect on the negotiation and coalition strategies that its members employ. As was mentioned in Chapter 1, the negotiating culture of the GATT led developing countries to label the institution a 'rich man's club'. Rather than expend limited resources in a forum that seemed weighted against them, developing countries successfully lobbied for the creation of a different economic organization that attached primacy to their development concerns – the UNCTAD. Their dealings with the GATT were marginal, and even these limited dealings were couched in a confrontational discourse. The expansion in the agenda of the WTO and its legalization has led developing countries to recognize that they can no longer afford to stand at the margins. However, the similarities between the organizational cultures of the GATT and the WTO have persisted through the continuities in decision-making procedures as well as the informal protocols of interaction in the Green Room and corridors. This has led developing countries to adhere, in general, to many of the negotiation strategies that they pursued in the GATT.

John Odell conceptualizes negotiation strategies across a

spectrum that ranges from value-claiming to value-creating: He writes:

> At one pole is the pure value-claiming or distributive strategy, a set of actions that promote the attainment of one party's goals when they are in conflict with those of the other party. . . . At the opposite pole is the pure integrative or value-creating strategy. It involves actions that promote the attainment of goals that are not in fundamental conflict – actions designed to expand rather than split the pie.

Along this spectrum, many developing countries in the WTO have tended to adopt the strict distributive strategy. Of course, this tendency has several sources including the role of the particular negotiator, the domestic political economy, and the political culture of the country. But there are two additional factors – both relating to the culture of the WTO – that further prompt developing countries to adopt hard-line positions and show limited flexibility in arriving at a compromise. First, the use of the strict distributive strategy is especially common when levels of trust among the negotiating parties are low, and such a situation exists in the WTO. Developing countries have long been resentful of the relative ease with which developed countries, both in the GATT and the WTO, have been able to bludgeon them into consensus, and keep expanding the agenda of the organization despite the reservations that developing countries have consistently had with this. Second, as was outlined in the previous section of this chapter, developing countries find themselves poorly equipped to deal with the technicalities of the negotiations, whereas integrative strategies require considerable knowledge and skill. The pace of the negotiations makes it especially difficult for developing countries to adopt proactive, positive negotiating positions, let alone formulate fallback positions that form an essential part of an integrative strategy. Often, they end up succumbing to pressure in the endgame and gain few concessions. Former Indian Ambassador B. L. Das comments on this negotiating trajectory of developing countries:

The transition from the long period of determined opposition to sudden collapse into acquiescence at the end has denied these countries the opportunity of getting anything in return for the concessions they finally make in the negotiations.

Agreements thus arrived at further exacerbate the level of distrust and endanger their political sustainability.

Finally, any discussion about the norms of negotiation in the WTO will be incomplete without a mention of the accession process. The WTO began with a membership of 128 members; its membership had expanded to 148 by 2005. The few remaining outside are lining up to join the club. The accession process, however, is not an easy one. It begins as a bilateral process, in which all interested members can make demands of the aspirant member, and the accession eventually has to be approved by a two-thirds majority. Acceding countries cannot negotiate concessions beyond those covered by the WTO agreements, but they may be asked by member countries to surrender much more. The accession of Cambodia in 2003 – the first Least Developed Country (LDC) to join the WTO since its creation in 1995 – provides a good example of how asymmetric this process can be. An Oxfam report points out that Cambodia was required to give up the use of generic medicines as part of its accession package, even though the WTO actually exempts LDCs from implementing this part of the agreement on intellectual property rights until 2016. In agriculture, the EU and the US have tariff peaks which are several times higher than those that Cambodia signed on to. Unsurprisingly, the Cambodian Minister of Commerce, Mr Cham Prasidh, is quoted as saying: 'This is a package of concessions and commitments that goes far beyond what is commensurate with the level of development of an LDC like Cambodia.'

This highly asymmetric accession process notwithstanding, countries have shown a willingness to give up rather a lot to acquire membership of the WTO. This is because members assume that the costs of accession, as well as some questionable decision-making procedures and politicized negotiation processes, will be easily outweighed by the benefits of belonging to the WTO. The expected benefits for developing countries (and indeed, most of the recent accessions have been developing countries) include MFN-based market access with all the other members, the protection of rules against the whims of the powerful, and an enforceable dispute-settlement mechanism to uphold that protection. Whether these benefits are actually as high as expected can perhaps be best gauged by examining the substance of the agreements.

Chapter 4
The expanding mandate

We saw in Chapters 2 and 3 that the structures and processes that underlie the workings of the WTO bear a close resemblance to those of the GATT. However, in the expanse and reach of its mandate, the WTO legislates and adjudicates in areas that go well beyond the border measures that concerned its predecessor. The central preoccupation of the GATT (as its name indicated) was with tariffs and other related border measures that applied to trade in goods; the agreements of the WTO cover tariffs, but also non-tariff barriers to trade, and extend into the areas of services and intellectual property rights. Many of these agreements take the organization into areas that have traditionally fallen within the domestic jurisdictions of states. In this chapter, I analyse the mandate of the WTO through an overview of its agreements. Regulation in some of these areas is inevitably a product of globalization that generates new problems, which necessitate international cooperation. However, their apparently technocratic and abstruse content notwithstanding, rule-making in the WTO is fundamentally a political process. The choice of what gets included in the agreements and what gets excluded is influenced critically by the interests of the powerful. The impact of these agreements has also often proven to be asymmetric, with many of the promised benefits for developing countries remaining unrealized.

The structure of the agreements

The agreements of the WTO are a product of the negotiations of the Uruguay Round that was completed in 1994 at Marrakesh. Legally overarching the set of all the agreements, which together number over 550 pages of printed text, is the Agreement establishing the WTO. There are four key annexes to the main agreement that contain the substance of the rules and commitments that members must abide by. Annex 1 has three parts that cover goods, services and intellectual property rights respectively. Contained within this first annex are also the schedules of commitments taken on by each member country that extend to over 30,000 printed pages! Annex 2 and 3 are on the Dispute Settlement Understanding and the Trade Policy Review Mechanism. Finally, Annex 4 covers the four plurilateral agreements, i.e. agreements signed by sub-sets of the entire membership. Besides these, several other legal texts have been added to the repertoire of agreements since 1994 such as the protocols on accession, the International Technology Agreement and the understanding on financial services. In this chapter, we will focus specifically on the three pillars of Annex 1, though some mention will be made of some of the plurilateral agreements. Annexes 2 and 3 are analysed in the next chapter.

The only substantive overlap between the agreements of the WTO and the preceding GATT regime is Annex 1A, i.e. the agreement dealing with trade in goods. This agreement is known as GATT 1994, and should not be confused with GATT 1947, which was a more limited agreement in the coverage of its multilateral disciplines. GATT 1947 dealt mainly with tariff barriers to trade in goods. The GATT's foray into non-tariff barriers had been through voluntary plurilateral codes of the Kennedy and Tokyo Rounds. The WTO integrates these multiple disciplines into the Single Undertaking by incorporating them in the multilateral rules of GATT 1994. As a result, GATT 1994 plunges into areas that lay outside the direct purview of GATT 1947 such as technical barriers to trade, government procurement, anti-dumping, customs

2. Structure of the WTO agreements

Umbrella	Agreement establishing the WTO		
	Goods (Annex 1a)	Services (Annex 1b)	Intellectual Property (Annex 1c)
Basic principles	GATT	GATS	TRIPs
Additional details	Other goods, agreements, and annexes	Services Annexes	
Market access commitments	Countries' schedules of commitments	Countries' schedules of commitments and MFN exemptions	
Dispute settlement	Dispute settlement Annex 2		
Transparency	Trade Policy Reviews Annex 3		
Plurilateral agreements	Trade in civil aircraft Government procurement Dairy products Bovine meat		

valuation and so forth. While the original GATT dealt with trade in goods, Annexes 1b and 1c – products of the Uruguay Round negotiations – bring the new areas of services and intellectual property rights within the mandate of the WTO. As the main barriers to trade in these so-called 'new issues' of the Uruguay Round – are not border measures but non-tariff barriers associated with domestic regulation, their inclusion within the WTO takes the organization firmly inside the terrain of domestic governance. The WTO retains many of the structures and procedures of its predecessor, but its regulations go into areas that the GATT never did, nor was intended to.

The reasons for this dramatic switch in the mandate of the WTO from the GATT model can be found in two phenomena. The first was the shift in the production patterns and comparative advantage of the developed countries, beginning with the US, from production of industrial products to services and intellectual property rights. It was inevitable that any trade organization, to sustain the commitment of the developed countries, would have to cover issues that were of paramount interest to them. The agenda of the Uruguay Round was driven by this evolving comparative advantage of the developed world. In the 1980s, the 'GATT bicycle theory' – attributed to economist Fred Bergsten – was commonly cited: if the GATT bicycle did not continue to move forward, it would topple over. The expanded WTO agenda may thus be seen as part of the same process of adaptation to the changing comparative advantage of member countries.

The second reason for the wider mandate of the WTO lay in the very achievements of the GATT, which had been extremely successful in the reduction of tariffs on industrial products. But as tariff barriers were prohibited, countries began to resort to non-tariff forms of protectionism. Robert Baldwin, in an oft-quoted and memorable analogy, has thus likened trade liberalization to draining a swamp: as successful pumping efforts leads to a fall in the water level (tariffs), they also reveal rocks, stumps and other obstacles (non-tariff barriers) that lie below the surface. To clear this drained land necessitates intrusions into the domestic regulatory regimes of member states. From this perspective, the expansion in the agenda of the WTO represents little more than the next and inevitable step in the process of trade liberalization. That expansion of the WTO's agenda, however, did not determine the actual content of its rules. In the following sections, I argue that exactly what gets regulated and with whose rules depends considerably on the power balances in the WTO and further affect inequality and marginalization within the organization.

The Multilateral Agreement on Trade in Goods/ GATT 1994

GATT 1994 builds on GATT 1947 and continues to deal with reductions in the barriers – tariffs and non-tariffs – to trade in goods. It includes the general rules that are to be applied to trade in goods, and contains the detailed schedules of commitments by individual countries on tariff reductions and bindings. Its general disciplines cover areas such as Most Favoured Nation (MFN) status, national treatment, customs valuation, elimination of quantitative restrictions, and emergency actions to restrict imports. To paraphrase Bernard Hoekman and Michel Kostecki, three purposes underlie the multitudinous and complex articles and agreements of the GATT: the establishment of non-discrimination, the prohibition of quantitative restrictions (QRs), and the prevention of the circumvention of the non-discrimination principle and other commitments that countries have agreed to abide by. Given the successes of GATT 1947 in achieving the first two goals, many of the articles and agreements of GATT 1994 provide ways of ensuring that the successes of the old GATT are not undone through non-tariff barriers.

The reason why GATT 1994 was able to emerge at all in its impressive, expansive form lies in the negotiated compromise of the Uruguay Round. GATT 1994, with its tariff bindings, coverage of non-tariff barriers, and stringent transparency requirements formed part of the so-called 'Grand Bargain' of the Uruguay Round of trade negotiations. Developing countries agreed to accept considerably more rigorous disciplines that extended into the domestic domain and into new areas that went considerably beyond the traditional sector of goods as the next sections illustrate. In return, they were promised that their major concerns would be included in the new regime. Admittedly, some rumblings of scepticism were heard at the time of signing the agreements; ten years after Marrakesh, even former enthusiasts for the agreements have begun to recognize that developing countries were short-changed. Below we examine who gave up what in the Grand Bargain so that the world could get a world trade organization.

Tariffs and trade

Tariffs represent a frequently used form of protectionism. Most economists regard tariffs as a preferable form of trade restriction to quotas. This is because quotas tend to be arbitrary, sever the link between domestic and foreign prices, and increase rent-seeking and corruption in the domestic economy. As a result, GATT 1947 and 1994 devote considerable attention to this subject. Article XI of the GATT requires a general elimination of quantitative restrictions; tariffs are permitted. Bernard Hoekman and Michel Kostecki identify two basic WTO rules for tariffs. First, tariffs must be non-discriminatory as per the MFN clause that was discussed in the previous chapter. Second, countries are not allowed to raise tariffs above the levels that they have committed to in the schedules, that is, they cannot raise tariffs beyond the 'tariff binding'. A 'positive list' approach is used in the schedules. This means that bindings apply only on those specific products that countries include in their schedules.

One of the many achievements of the Uruguay Round was to expand the number of products on which tariffs were bound, and also the number of countries that took on such bindings. Until the Uruguay Round, former colonies had acceded to the GATT without tariff negotiations, while Special and Differential treatment further exempted them from submitting tariff schedules. The creation of the WTO completely transformed this, as all WTO members were required to submit tariff schedules. Developing countries proved amenable to this change as a result of the Grand Bargain. They were promised tariff reductions in Northern markets in products in which developing countries had a comparative advantage. One such issue was agriculture, which had effectively been excluded from GATT rules in the past. Under GATT 1994, members were obliged to bind 100% of their agricultural tariff lines. The agreement also promised an end to the exceptionalism granted to textiles and clothing through a phase-out of the Multi Fibre Agreement. In return for these gains, developing countries bound their tariffs. Hoekman and Kostecki record that prior to the Uruguay Round, only 22% of industrial products from developing countries were bound. Post Uruguay Round, this figure had risen to 72%. Developed countries, in turn, took their own commitments on industrial products even further, increasing the share of their bound industrial tariff lines from 78% to 99%.

A closer look at these tariff bindings, however, reveals several problems. The increase in tariff bindings taken on by developing countries was massive, but it did not result in a commensurate level of actual liberalization. This is because developing countries had bound their tariffs at levels that were significantly higher than their applied tariffs. As a result, the bindings did not improve market access within developing countries; their only substantive achievement was to establish a ceiling, above which the particular country could not easily raise tariffs without justification. These effectively limited schedules of developing countries have naturally provoked the ire of countries, practitioners, and theoreticians. The continued trade restrictions of developing countries appear especially offensive to some, given that average applied tariff rates on industrial products have fallen below 3% in developed countries. Some liberal economists have been quick to argue that developing countries must engage in some real liberalization now before demanding any further concessions from the developed world. But the schedules of the developed countries too, in spite of impressive averages, are far from perfect.

Averages of lower tariffs on industrial goods conceal the very high 'tariff peaks' that developed countries continue to maintain on select products, many of which constitute the key export interests of developing countries, such as leather, rubber, and footwear. Textiles and agriculture, in which several developing countries enjoy an export advantage, had been effectively excluded from general GATT rules through exceptions and waivers; one of the main achievements of the Uruguay Round was the inclusion of these issues into the WTO. But even though the Multi Fibre Agreement was scheduled for a complete phase-out by 2005, tariffs of the developed countries on textiles remained very high. For instance, US tariffs on about 52% of products in textiles and clothing ranged from 15 to 35%. Other sectors in which developing countries enjoy a comparative advantage, such as tropical products and fish, face similarly high barriers to market access in developed countries. In other words, despite the fact that tariff reductions on goods enjoy a fifty-year legacy from the GATT, the process of multilateral tariff reduction within WTO auspices remains severely unbalanced against the weaker players in the international system.

Besides having to contend with tariff peaks that are effectively permitted in the WTO, developing countries also face the problem of 'tariff escalation', that is tariff structures wherein raw materials are charged lower duties than processed products. Such tariff structures create a disincentive against the processing of primary commodities in developing countries. Though tariff escalation has declined as a result of the Uruguay Round negotiations, the problem continues in some of the areas where developing countries enjoy potential strength and thwarts their economic development. Similarly, even though quotas were always prohibited in the GATT, countries managed to find devices to use them. Article XI of GATT 1994 disallows quotas, but tariff quotas have proliferated in the key area of agriculture. As a result of the prevalence of tariff peaks, tariff escalations, and tariff quotas, developing countries find that the benefits of the Uruguay Round have fallen far short of the estimates (e.g. through studies conducted by the World Bank and the GATT Secretariat) when they signed on to the agreements. The unfulfilled promises of the Uruguay Round have attracted considerable rancour from developing countries and formed a major part of the agenda of coalitions of developing countries at the Seattle and Doha Ministerial conferences in 1999 and 2001 respectively.

Agriculture and textiles

Nowhere are the problems of unfulfilled promises more apparent than in the area of agriculture and textiles. The inclusion of these two sectors within GATT 1994 formed the key component of the deal that was offered to developing countries. However, GATT 1994 does not include these two sectors within its general rules; rather, they form a part of a set of sector-specific agreements where the general rules do not actually apply.

The Agreement on Agriculture was a product of the concerted efforts of a coalition of developed and developing countries known as the Cairns Group, besides the ultimate compromise between the EU and the US (see box). The Agreement targets 'three pillars' of agricultural trade policy: market access, domestic support mechanisms, and export subsidies. In addition to these instruments, the agreement also addresses the non-tariff barriers of arbitrary standards that countries might employ in the Agreement on Sanitary and Phytosanitary Measures (SPS) (discussed later in this section). Some of these commitments, at first glance, appear quite radical, especially if one also incorporates the transparency gains that should have emerged as a result of the process of 'tariffication', that is the conversion of quotas and other protectionist devices into tariffs.

The Cairns Group

The inclusion of agriculture into the Uruguay Round was historic, and the role of the Cairns Group in brokering the deal has attracted considerable attention. The Cairns Group of Agricultural Exporting Countries was formed in 1986, with an initial membership comprising Argentina, Australia,

Brazil, Canada, Chile, Colombia, Fiji, Hungary, Indonesia, Malaysia, New Zealand, the Philippines, Thailand, and Uruguay. It differed from many coalitions in the past in that it was an issue-specific coalition and combined developed and developing countries. The group arose in response to the agricultural subsidies war that had arisen between the EU and the US, which was eroding the comparative advantage of middle-income agricultural exporters who could not offer competing levels of subsidy for their own producers.

Having successfully engineered the inclusion of agriculture on the agenda of the new round, the group acted as a mediating coalition between the two policy extremes advocated by the EU and the US. While presenting itself as a negotiating coalition with a positive agenda (as opposed to blocking coalitions that developing countries had traditionally formed), it was also willing to use the threat to block when necessary. When the Agreement on Agriculture was finally included within the Marrakesh Agreement, many observers attributed this achievement to the negotiating efforts of the Cairns Group. For almost a decade thereafter, the Cairns Group was held up as a model coalition, prompting a series of coalition attempts emulating its 'issue-based diplomacy'.

These experiments with issue-based coalitions emulating the Cairns Group generated mixed results. This is because the Cairns Group was a product of some irreproducible conditions that included the unsustainably costly subsidies war, which even the EU and the US wanted to bring into control. Further, the Cairns Group shared its long-term objectives with the US at the time of the Uruguay Round. Finally, most analyses focusing on the successes of the Cairns Group ignore the marginalization of the group in the endgame. The final deal was struck in the Blair House accord between the US and the EU in 1992, in which the Cairns Group was completely sidelined. Given that the deal on agriculture was

New export subsides were prohibited by the agreement. To improve market access, all agricultural tariffs had to be bound. In certain products where some countries had bound their tariffs at prohibitively high levels, minimum market access commitments were ensured by setting Tariff Rate Quotas (TRQs). Recall that quotas are otherwise prohibited in the GATT. But in agriculture, a certain quota of imports was negotiated as mandatory in areas where countries had bound tariffs to prohibitively high levels (e.g. Japan's tariff policy on rice), so that some imports were allowed market access at a lower tariff rate. On domestic support measures (which tend to encourage over-production and thereby introduce distortions in international markets), an Aggregate Measure of Support (AMS) was negotiated. The AMS is calculated using the base years of 1986 to 1988 and is used to assess how much domestic support countries are providing for the agricultural sector. It categorizes subsidies into four boxes, thereby allowing some and completely prohibiting others. This is because the AMS is not targeted towards all agricultural policy reform; its purpose is only to address those policies that have a trade-distorting effect. As per this logic, domestic support measures in the Red Box are prohibited. The Amber Box measures are to be cut as per the rates shown in the previous table. The Green Box allows the use of domestic support measures such as government-funded research, direct income transfers for farmers that are not coupled with production, and food security.

An additional Blue Box was negotiated as part of the Blair House deal between the US and the EU, which allowed EU compensation payments for farmers required to limit production and US deficiency payments. The Agreement also specified the cuts that had to be made in export subsidies; new export subsidies were prohibited. The obligations on developing countries, particularly Least Developing Countries (LDCs), given especially the concerns of food-importing countries at the time of the Uruguay Round negotiations, were considerably weaker than those that had been placed upon the developed countries. Finally, it looked like developing countries had got themselves quite a bargain.

A closer inspection reveals that the liberalization process itself remained quite conservative. As with manufactures, tariffs were bound at significantly higher levels than the applied rates, producing the 'binding overhang.' As tariff reductions per item had to meet a minimum of 15%, developed countries could concentrate reductions in areas of little importance to developing countries and still meet the required average of 36% overall reduction in six years. Similarly, as a concession to the EU in the Blair House accord, it was agreed that the AMS would not be product specific. As a result, developed countries were able to meet the required cuts in domestic support by focusing on areas that were of no major consequence for developing countries. Agriculture still remains a significantly more protected sector in developed countries than manufactures. T. Hertel and W. Martin estimate in a study published in 2000 that the farm policies of developed countries cause annual welfare losses of US$40 billion for developing countries. The Agreement on Agriculture did have a 'built-in agenda' that was to be launched in 2000, but agricultural liberalization remains an acrimonious and fraught process (to be discussed further in Chapter 6).

The Agreement on Textiles and Clothing (ATC) has also not delivered the expected benefits. As a result of the import restrictions by developed countries in this sector, developing countries continue to incur annual welfare losses of about US$10 billion. The persistence of such losses might at first glance seem surprising, especially as the ATC stipulated that the system of quotas under the Multi Fibre Agreement would be phased out in four phases over a ten-year period. But lack of specification on exactly what gets liberalized when has allowed developed countries to reserve the liberalization of some of the most important items for developing countries to the last phase, that is the end of 2004. As a result, many of the benefits that were supposed to have accrued in the first decade of the WTO, and thereby provide a balance against the costs that developing countries bore through the inclusion of issues such as intellectual property rights, investment measures, and services, have not materialized.

Rules, regulations, and non-tariff barriers

While benefits of GATT 1994 have remained unrealized, the costs of implementing the agreement have increased with the creation of a more rigorous and intrusive set of rules. Some of these rules overlapped with those that dated back to the Tokyo Round and were devised to address the issue of proliferating non-tariff barriers. But GATT 1994 bound all members to these rules, in contrast to the Tokyo Round, which only had voluntary codes on these matters. Further, the content of these obligatory standards usually conforms to the standards of the developed countries rather than the indigenous standards of developing countries. J. Michael Finger and Philip Schuler thus argue in a World Bank study that the content of agreements like the customs valuation agreement, agreement on sanitary and phytosanitary barriers to trade (SPS), and the TRIPs agreement amounts to developed countries saying to the others, "Do it my way!" These standards are hence often seen as an imposition from the developed countries, via the WTO. Even if their economies might benefit from the infrastructural reform that these agreements require in the long run, developing countries resent the costs that they incur in their implementation. The creation of these rules, as a result, has not only expanded the mandate of the WTO considerably beyond the structures of the GATT, but it has also exacerbated North-South antagonisms in the WTO. It is true that these agreements do allow longer transition periods to developing countries. However, particularly since the Seattle Ministerial Conference, developing countries have argued that the costs of implementation are far higher than the breathing time that the transition periods allow them to cover.

The agreement on customs valuation in GATT 1994 is an example of this genre of agreements. The possibility that countries would apply arbitrary standards on imported goods for customs purposes, and thereby undo the benefits of tariff reductions with a non-tariff barrier, was quite high. The customs valuation code was formulated to address this risk, and was integrated into GATT 1994 to supersede the vague customs valuation requirements of GATT 1947. The agreement requires members to bring their customs regulations in line with a set of agreed standards for the valuation of imports for customs purposes. As the customs administration procedures of the developed countries are already well established, developing countries bear the brunt of the reforms. These reform costs are often very high. For instance, Finger and Schuler provide a conservative estimate that the costs of implementing the customs valuation agreement for Jamaica will be US$840,000 (to cover training costs of $120,000, computing equipment and database costs of $150,000, and increased staffing costs of $600,000).

The Agreement on the Application of Sanitary and Phytosanitary (SPS) Measures – that was negotiated as a part of the Agreement on Agriculture, which falls within GATT 1994 – poses problems similar to those described in the case of customs valuation. The agreement was formulated 'to maintain the sovereign right of any government to provide the level of health protection it deems appropriate, but to ensure that these sovereign rights are not misused for protectionist purposes and do not result in unnecessary barriers to international trade.' In principle, this does not amount to a harmonization of standards; countries are allowed to maintain whatever standards and methods of assessment they prefer. But if it applies those standards at its borders on incoming goods, the SPS agreement does require the country to demonstrate their scientific basis. As the existing internationally recognized standards are those that were evolved by developed countries, the burden of proving that indigenous standards are equally effective is an onerous one for developing countries. Even if their systems might have been working effectively and efficiently in the past, developing countries end up investing very large sums of money into modifying their own standards to bring them in line with those of the developed countries. For instance, Finger and Schuler record that Argentina spent over US$80 million to establish greater levels of animal and plant sanitation; in some cases, the costs of implementation can exceed the annual development budget of Least Developed Countries (LDCs). The Agreement on Technical Barriers to Trade (TBT) poses similar difficulties for developing countries.

Not only can agreements like the SPS and TBT be costly to implement, but their rules intrude into national regulatory regimes, ethics, consumer choice and cultural habits of people. The dispute between the US and the EU over the EU's import ban on beef that had been treated with hormones proved so trenchant precisely because it had an impact on the food habits and cultural preferences of people. The WTO Dispute Settlement Panel and subsequently the Appellate Body ruled against the ban on the grounds that it had violated the SPS requirement on scientific justification of national norms and the use of risk assessment procedures developed by relevant international organizations. When the EU announced that it was unable to comply with the ruling, a WTO arbitration panel authorized retaliation by the US and subsequently by Canada. The case was seen as symbolic of the WTO's intrusive capacity into national preferences and local food habits.

Another contested area where new intrusions into the domestic terrain were made by the GATT as a result of the Uruguay Round was that of Trade Related Investment Measures (TRIMs). TRIMs are policies used by governments that require foreign investors to meet certain performance standards in order to boost their domestic economies in a particular way. Examples include local content requirements (whereby investors must use a certain minimum of domestically produced inputs), export requirements (multinational enterprises must export a certain proportion of their produce to improve the balance of payments position of the country), or technology transfer requirements. Developing countries had actively resisted their inclusion into the GATT, claiming that these issues took the GATT outside its original mandate. As a result of this opposition, the TRIMs agreement did not go as far as the US would have liked, and developing countries further won the benefit of longer periods of implementation. But it did become an integral part of GATT 1994. The agreement disallows measures against foreign investors and foreign products that are inconsistent with the GATT's national treatment obligation and the ban on Quantitative Restrictions.

Akin to the agreements on SPS, TBT, and the other new issues, the push for TRIMs came from the developed world. And just as the SPS and TBT agreements apply Northern standards, the TRIMs agreement is designed to protect foreign direct investment (mainly Northern investment) in host countries (predominantly Southern countries). Even these asymmetries within the WTO agenda would have been acceptable, if they were balanced by other agreements or clauses that protected interests in the developing world as per the Grand Bargain. However, this is seldom the case. For instance, even though the interests of foreign investors are safeguarded through the TRIMs, the interests of the host country are not. Hence even though TRIMs effectively introduces a code of conduct for the host country towards multinational corporations (MNCs), the idea for a UN Code on Conduct for Transnational Corporations, which developing countries had lobbied for, proved to be a non-starter and was finally scuttled in 1991.

While the scope and reach of GATT 1994 is considerably more expansive and intrusive than GATT 1947, this should not be interpreted to mean that countries are defenceless against the advancing juggernaut of international regulation. A temporary suspension of obligations is possible under a variety of provisions including Anti-Dumping (ADs), Countervailing Duties (CVDs), Balance of Payments, infant industry protection, emergency safeguards, and special safeguards that are allowed in agriculture and textiles. Some of these provisions also existed in the old GATT but were seldom used. This is because countries, especially large countries, found it easier to impose the so-called bilaterally negotiated 'voluntary export restraints' (VERs). The achievement of the WTO was to prohibit VERs and specify the conditions under which obligations could be legally suspended; the fact that these agreements could be enforced under the WTO's Dispute Settlement Mechanism gave them added teeth. In practice, however, it has proven difficult to prevent countries – developed and developing – from abusing some of these provisions and undermining the concessions that have been so laboriously negotiated.

One of the most frequently used (and abused) provisions of the WTO to suspend MFN obligations is Anti-Dumping (AD). Dumping is said to occur if 'a company exports a product at a price lower than the price it normally charges in its own home market.' Governments in the WTO are allowed to act against such dumping, but they must be able to show that dumping is causing or threatening to cause 'material injury' to the competing domestic industry. The Agreement on Anti-Dumping is a highly abstruse one and countries are wont to use it far more frequently and easily than can be justified in economic or legal terms. While the main users of AD have traditionally been developed countries, by 1996 developing countries had overtaken developed ones as initiators of AD investigations. In contrast, most provisions allowing the temporary suspension of duties, including emergency safeguard provisions and CVDs, remain surprisingly under-utilized.

Two explanations seem plausible for the frequent resort to AD actions by WTO members. First, AD duties are the easiest to slap on another country, given especially the abstruse nature of the agreement and difficulties in calculating the extent of dumping; the other provisions are clearer and are hence less conducive to abuse. For instance, the emergency safeguards provisions are less easily used due to the strict criteria for their application and associated compensation that may be demanded of the country employing the safeguard; AD actions are easier to employ. Second, the absolute increase in the use of escape mechanisms to circumvent obligations may be related to the expanded scope of WTO regulations and their enforceability. Rather than risk retaliation through rule violation, it seems likely that countries would resort to any manner of devices to preemptively claim inability to abide by their commitments. AD duties provide precisely such a means by claiming that a trading partner is 'unfairly' dumping low-priced products into the domestic economy. The incentive to resort to such measures was small when the GATT restricted itself to tariffs on certain goods; but GATT 1994 and accompanying agreements regulate in areas that matter and on which retaliation will hurt. This raises the bigger question: has the expansion in the agenda of the WTO also enhanced the scope for rule circumvention on a scale that might undermine the entire WTO system? This widening and deepening of the WTO agenda is evident in the agreements on services and intellectual property.

The General Agreement on Trade in Services (GATS)

The idea of including trade in services within the GATT was first proposed by the US at the GATT's ministerial conference in 1982. The push for this inclusion was driven in good measure by the changing comparative advantage of the developed countries. By 1981, for instance, services had come to comprise about 66% of the GDP of developed countries and 67% of their employment. It was inevitable that if the commitment of the developed countries to the GATT was to be maintained, multilateral trade liberalization under the GATT would have to be extended to areas where the proactive export interests of the developed countries lay.

But the entry of services into the GATT proved difficult. For a treaty that had dealt entirely with trade in goods, services presented a qualitatively new issue. The services sector had, in fact, been traditionally thought of as comprising 'non-tradables'. It covered a great diversity of activities and required methods of supply that differed radically from goods. In several sub-sectors, for instance, provision of services requires proximity between the seller and consumer (e.g. coiffure, restaurants and hotel industry), requiring the movement of consumers (e.g. tourists) or sellers establishing commercial presence in the host country (foreign direct investment). Many are tailored to the specific needs of customers and lack the level of standardization that is common to goods. Any liberalization of this sector cannot be conducted through simple tariff reductions, and requires a modification of domestic regulations on matters that affect the movements of goods, people and capital. Many developing countries feared that the international regulation of this crucial services sector would jeopardize their sovereignty. They were also concerned that the inclusion of services in the GATT would divert attention from issues that affected them, such as the proliferation of VERs and non-tariff barriers. Finally while both developed and developing countries were unclear about the implications of including services within the GATT, they recognized that the services sector held the key to the health of their national economies. Concessions on an area of such great importance could not be frivolously bartered. The attempt by the US to introduce services into the GATT agenda immediately galvanized developing countries into a blocking coalition of over 61 countries.

The story of the inclusion of the services into the GATT, in its first part at least, is not a heartening one. In the face of the resistance from many countries, a 'compromise' was reached at the 1982 ministerial: a work programme on services was initiated, which would allow the GATT and its contracting parties to prepare a technical base for negotiations in this sector. Another similar 'compromise', in spite of the long-standing opposition of the coalition of the G10 (comprising Argentina, Brazil, Egypt, India and Yugoslavia, along with Cuba, Nicaragua, Nigeria, Tanzania and Peru), was effected at the Punta del Este meeting. A counter-coalition had come to support the US agenda, now supported by other developed countries, and services were included into the Uruguay Round agenda. Developing countries, however, were able to obtain the concession that cross-issue linkages would be avoided through the dual-track mechanism. Yet another 'compromise' and though the negotiations on services continued on a different track from goods, the General Agreement on Trade in Services was firmly integrated within the WTO agreements and within the Single Undertaking. Still hoping to make the best of future services negotiations, developing countries attempted to restrict the mode of supply that dealt with direct commercial presence. They were unsuccessful in this attempt; their more positive attempts to ensure that developed countries made some genuine commitments on imports of services supplied through the movement of labour have yielded only minimal results so far. In retrospect, given that developing countries got little of concrete value in textiles and agriculture, some might argue that they had conceded rather a lot on services for nothing in return.

In theory, the inclusion of services within the GATS in the WTO presents a massive jump in the mandate of the organization, especially as barriers to trade in services can be removed only through modification of domestic regulatory regimes. For instance, a discussion of minimum standards is inevitable if a country is to allow an influx of doctors and nurses from another country with a different education system. In practice, however, the GATS is quite a limited agreement. In structure the agreement is similar to GATT 1994 and comprises a set of general principles and rules, specific commitments that apply to sub-sectors listed in Members' schedules, and annexes dealing with specific sectors. Article 1 defines the scope of GATS and its application to all four modes of supply: cross-border supply (i.e. not requiring the movement of supplier or consumer), movement of the consumer, commercial presence, and supply through the temporary movement of natural persons. Similar to the Agreement on Agriculture in the GATT, GATS has a Built-In Agenda for successive negotiations. It resembles the GATT in its reliance on non-discrimination as its first and foremost principle. But due to the preference of the EU and developing countries for an agreement with softer obligations, non-discrimination in the GATS is more circumscribed than non-discrimination in the GATT. MFN is a general obligation (Article II), but members are allowed to list MFN exemptions. National treatment (Article XVII) is a specific obligation rather than a general one, which means that it applies to only those services specified in Members' schedules as per the listed qualifications. Governments remain free to set standards and qualification requirements, so long as the same regulations apply to foreign suppliers as national ones. GATS also contains a market access obligation (Article XVI), which in principle disallows six kinds of market access restrictions, though countries can list specific restrictions within these categories in particular sectors if they so wish. Unlike other international agreements like the North Atlantic Free Trade Agreement, most obligations in the GATS operate through a 'positive list'. This means that disciplines apply only in the specific areas and extent made by each individual member.

There are four annexes or special agreements attached to GATS: Movement of Natural Persons, Financial Services, Telecommunications and Air Transport Services. The first of these annexes has aroused considerable acrimony from developing countries that enjoy a comparative advantage in the export of services through Mode 4. Commitments of the developed countries to the import of services through Mode 4 are few; non-tariff barriers persist in the form of Economic Needs Tests; while the Annex on the Movement of Natural Persons further specifies that

GATS deals only with the temporary movement of people rather than immigration. The inadequacy of commitments in this Annex is now widely recognized, and at least some of the concerns of developing countries have been carried over into the current round of trade negotiations, addressed in Chapter 6. Financial services and telecommunications were included in separate annexes in the GATS. This was mainly because the US was dissatisfied with the concessions that other countries had made in these areas; the deadlines for completing these negotiations were thus postponed beyond the Marrakesh deadline. Having separate annexes on these sectors further provided a way of ensuring sectoral reciprocity in these key areas. Negotiations in financial services and telecommunications were completed by December 1997 and February 1997 respectively.

While the inclusion of services within the GATT agenda may have been a contested process initially, several developing countries have now begun to realize their potential as exporters of services. The re-location of call centres from Western Europe to developing countries like India is one example; the emergence of India as a major exporter of software is another. Further, developing countries have also begun to play an active and successful role as agenda-setters in the GATS. For instance, in the first phase of the Built-In Agenda, members were required to collectively formulate a set of guidelines and procedures for subsequent negotiations by 2001. A coalition of twenty-four developing countries was formed in 1999 to this end, and successfully shaped the Guidelines that have formed the basis for the current negotiations.

The Agreement on Trade-Related Intellectual Property Rights (TRIPs)

Besides GATS, the agreement on TRIPs was negotiated and signed at Marrkakesh. The inclusion and subsequent negotiation of TRIPs proved to be even more controversial than services, not least because it caught up popular imagination at an unprecedented level. The reason for this was partly that TRIPs required governments to modify their national legislation on patents, copyrights, and trademarks to bring them in line with the new agreement. But more importantly, the agreement applied to such basic and everyday necessities as medicines, and its application would affect the access of national populations to life-saving drugs and technologies. Ten years since it was signed, as countries and their populations begin to understand the nature of obligations that TRIPs demands, controversies and anger surrounding the agreement have not abated.

The idea of strengthening international legislation on intellectual property rights pre-dates the Uruguay Round. Most countries recognized that the provision of intellectual property in many of its forms (ideas, inventions, discoveries) suffers from a public goods problem, that is it is difficult to exclude those who did not bear the costs from benefiting from the rewards of production. The risk of free-riding would act as a deterrent to many crucial inventions and innovations. As a result, governments have always had some system of protecting intellectual property rights at home. Internationally, the World Intellectual Property Organization (WIPO), which has traditionally administered the many treaties that deal with different aspects of intellectual property rights (IPRs), was established in 1967.

Despite the existence of a network of arrangements to manage IPRs, the US and EU began to be increasingly concerned that their comparative advantage as exporters of intellectual property was being undermined by cheap counterfeits. The US attempts to include TRIPs within the purview of the GATT go back to the Tokyo Round. Developing countries, however, were opposed to this idea. They argued that any changes to international rules on IPRs should be conducted within an organization whose mandate was devoted exclusively to such issues, that is the WIPO. This opposition from developing countries was unsurprising, given that they were largely importers of IPRs and their IPR protection regimes were often weak. Their scepticism about including TRIPs within the GATT also found support in some economic and social arguments. Ann Capling, for instance, points out that many countries (including developed countries until recently) have afforded only weak patent protection for pharmaceuticals on the grounds that patent protection will inflate the prices of essential drugs. She further presents the case that 'Patent owners may place onerous conditions on the use of new technology, or may simply refuse to license new technology in order to preserve their monopolistic position,' thereby actually slowing 'the dissemination of new ideas, basic knowledge, and technological advancement' rather than encouraging them. That TRIPs was nonetheless included on the agenda of the Uruguay Round, and subsequently as an integral part of the WTO demands an explanation.

Besides the fact that the interests of the developed world (and their companies) were pushing for an expansion of the GATT in the direction of the 'new issues', three reasons help explain the inclusion of TRIPs in the WTO. First, by the late 1980s, concurrently with the negotiations, the US had begun to impose unilateral trade sanctions on developing countries for violating US patent law. The most dreaded of these was the Special 301 section of the Omnibus Trade and Competitiveness Act of 1988, by which the US Trade Representative would place countries with objectionable IPR regimes (e.g. Brazil and India, among others) on its "priority watch-list' and threaten them with unilateral trade sanctions. Faced with such threats, developing countries began to re-consider their opposition: including TRIPs within the multilateral system provided the possibility of curbing the 'aggressive unilateralism' of the US. Second, TRIPs formed a part of the Grand Bargain and developing countries were offered concessions in other issue-areas. But third, at least some developing country negotiators have revealed in subsequent interviews that the technicalities of TRIPs had evaded them at the time when the agreement was being negotiated. Rather, they had believed that the TRIPs agreement would be limited to counterfeit goods.

9. The inclusion of TRIPs into the GATT was a new development. Developing countries had not anticipated that the new agreement that was being negotiated under the auspices of the GATT would extend beyond the issue of counterfeits.

The Agreement that actually resulted at the end of the Uruguay Round was a highly complex one, comprising seven major parts and 73 articles. It extends to copyrights, trademarks, geographical indications, industrial designs, patents, lay-out designs of integrated circuits, and undisclosed information including trade secrets. The Agreement is based on the same principles of transparency and non-discrimination as the GATT, but further establishes minimum standards that countries must abide by in all the seven areas of IPRs. Most of these standards, akin to the standards set through the GATT, are based on the interests of developed countries. Developing countries were granted some concessions in the form of longer periods for implementation. However, these concessions have proved to be inadequate, given the costs of implementation that developing countries face. A few safeguards have been built into the TRIPs such as Article 8 on the right of governments to protect public health and even override patents if need be. In practice, developing countries have found it extremely difficult to make use of these safeguards. Some of the problems with the TRIPs agreement, particularly the costs of implementation of the agreement and its provisions on patents, were brought to the fore by developing countries and non-governmental organizations in the run-up to the Doha Ministerial Conference in 2001, and will be covered in Chapter 6.

All the agreements discussed in this chapter provide an insight into the expansive and complicated network of rules that comprise the WTO. The process of including new issues into the WTO continues unabated. There is a new round of trade negotiations currently underway, known as the Doha Development Agenda, which will address some of the problems associated with the current agreements but will inevitably take the WTO into newer terrain.

The widening and deepening of the reach of the WTO has not gone uncontested. Most of the agreements, arrived at through difficult compromise, have had to rely on ambiguities and inconsistencies to make the agreement palatable to all parties concerned. These political discrepancies within the agreements often carry over into the Dispute Settlement Mechanism and require legal resolution. In the next chapter, I examine the legal system that underpins the WTO as an international organization.

Chapter 5
Settling disputes

Many negotiators and scholars agree that while the achievements of the Uruguay Round negotiations were many, the jewel in the crown of these achievements is the powerful Dispute Settlement Understanding (DSU). The emergence of this powerful mechanism imparts an unprecedented level of legalization to the WTO. In a project on 'Legalization and International Politics', scholars led by Judith Goldstein, Miles Kahler, Robert Keohane, and Anne-Marie Slaughter analyse the concept of legalization across three key dimensions: obligation, precision, and delegation. In all three, the WTO is an exemplar. Its members are obliged to abide by its rules or face retaliation; its rules are precise and determine what may be expected of its members; and in the instance of disputes, members delegate the authority to settle these disputes to a Dispute Settlement Panel, an Appellate Body, and ultimately the Dispute Settlement Body. Through the DSU, the WTO has acquired teeth; its rules can be enforced with an automacity and with consequences that were quite alien to the GATT. These are major developments with system-wide consequences. They have deprived developed countries (particularly the US) of the excuse that the inadequacies and poor enforcement capacity of the GATT compelled them to resort to unilateral and bilateral measures. They have also imparted greater certainty and predictability to the international trading system, which are particularly valued by developing countries.

In this chapter, I examine dispute settlement within the WTO by focusing on its procedures and some of its landmark cases. As WTO law evolves, so does the legalism of the organization. But this chapter highlights two fundamental problems with this trend towards increasing legalization. First, the newfound legalism of WTO rules contrasts with the *ad hoc* and informal processes that actually create those rules (as discussed in Chapter 3). The disjuncture between the informal rule-making procedures of the WTO and the highly legal implementation of those rules underpins the challenges that the organization is facing from different fronts today. The WTO system risks an implosion if these discrepancies are not corrected. Second, despite their preference for a stronger rules-based system (which the DSU facilitates), developing countries in practice find themselves ill equipped to utilize this system to their advantage. In the context of these difficulties, the sustainability of the WTO system in its current form becomes even more suspect.

Dispute settlement in the WTO

Article XVI:1 of the Agreement establishing the WTO states that the WTO shall be guided by the 'decisions, procedures and customary practices' followed by GATT 1947. Despite this attempt to maintain a link with its predecessor, the DSU under the WTO presents a departure from the GATT in several important ways.

First, the DSU establishes a single unified dispute settlement system under the WTO, in contrast to the multiple dispute settlement procedures that came with the codes of the Tokyo Round. Exceptions to this are clearly listed in Annex 2.

Second, and very importantly, a considerable degree of automaticity has been introduced in the process that was non-existent in the GATT. This is because dispute settlement under the GATT worked on the principle of 'positive consensus', that is, any member – including the parties to the dispute – could initially block the establishment of a Panel or the subsequent adoption of the Panel

Report. In contrast, dispute settlement in the WTO works on the principle of 'negative consensus'. This means that after parties have unsuccessfully attempted to resolve their dispute through consultation, unless the Dispute Settlement Body (DSB) – the General Council by another name and comprising the entire membership of the WTO – decides by consensus *not* to allow the establishment of a Panel (Article VI) or to reject its decision (Article XVII:14), the Panel will be established. Similarly, a decision by the Panel (or the Appellate Body) requires consensus to be rejected. Panels are constituted by three or five 'well-qualified governmental and/or non-governmental individuals' (Article 8) drawn from a roster of potential panelists who are nominated by WTO members. The DSU provides clear terms of reference for the Panel on its *modus operandi*.

Third, the DSU establishes an appellate procedure in the WTO that did not exist in the GATT. John Jackson explains the introduction of the appellate procedure as a *quid pro quo* that was exchanged for the automaticity, through the negative consensus requirement, in the adoption of Panel decisions. The Appellate Body deals only with issues such as legal interpretation; it cannot re-examine the evidence or address new issues. The report of the Appellate Body is final, and must be adopted by the DSB unless a negative consensus prevails.

Fourth, the DSU provides for improved surveillance mechanisms for the implementation of DSB decisions that were virtually non-existent in the GATT. If the offending country fails to adopt corrective measures 'within a reasonable period of time', Article XXII.2 of the DSU requires the disputing parties to negotiate compensation for the aggrieved party. In the absence of agreement on this compensation, the DSB can authorize retaliation. The only way the DSB can reject this authorization is through consensus.

Finally, all the provisions of the DSU come with clearly specified time-frames for each stage (outlined in the flowchart). In the GATT,

3. Stages in the dispute settlement process

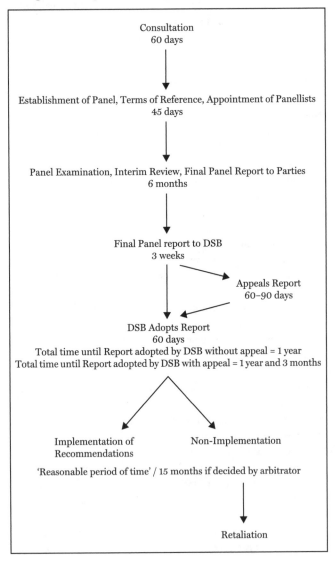

Consultation
60 days

Establishment of Panel, Terms of Reference, Appointment of Panellists
45 days

Panel Examination, Interim Review, Final Panel Report to Parties
6 months

Final Panel report to DSB
3 weeks

Appeals Report
60–90 days

DSB Adopts Report
60 days
Total time until Report adopted by DSB without appeal = 1 year
Total time until Report adopted by DSB with appeal = 1 year and 3 months

Implementation of
Recommendations

Non-Implementation

'Reasonable period of time' / 15 months if decided by arbitrator

Retaliation

cases could be indefinitely dragged out among the disputants, involving considerable costs for the aggrieved parties. These costs were of particular concern for developing countries, which remained wary of bringing disputes to the GATT even when there was a very high probability of the decision eventually turning out to be in their favour. In the WTO, not only are definite time limits attached to each stage of the dispute settlement process, but the process can be expedited if it involves perishable products and if developing countries are involved as complainants against developed countries.

While the DSU under the WTO is a considerably stronger instrument than the dispute settlement process of the GATT, the onus of employing this instrument falls on the members themselves. This is in keeping with the WTO's member-driven character and derives also from its GATT legacy. Member states need to exercise constant vigilance on how their interests are being affected by the trade policies of other members, as well as domestic awareness of WTO rules by companies and consumers who might be affected by rule violations. The rules of the WTO provide some assistance in the exercise of this vigilance through the requirement that all members publish their trade regulations, notify changes to the WTO, and respond to any requests by members for further information. Additionally, the WTO conducts periodic Trade Policy Reviews. Detailed provisions about the Trade Policy Review Mechanism (TPRM), which forms an integral part of the WTO, are listed in Annex 3. The top body for this exercise is the Trade Policy Review Body – the General Council by yet another name – but the Secretariat is responsible for conducting the reviews.

The TPRM has three goals. First, it attempts to ensure the transparency of Members' trade policies through regular monitoring. Second, it attempts to improve the quality of public and intergovernmental debate on the issues. Finally, it seeks to enable a multilateral assessment of the effects of policies on the world trading system. Each review comprises two documents – one prepared by the government concerned, and the other prepared by the WTO Trade Policies Review division. Countries with the largest trade shares are subject to the most frequent reviews, for example the Quad group (Canada, EU, Japan, and US) are reviewed every two years; the next 16 countries (in terms of shares of world trade) are reviewed every four years; while the Least Developed Countries (LDCs) enjoy much longer time periods (sometimes more than six years) between each review. Even a damning Trade Policy Review by the Secretariat, however, is not enough to initiate action by the Dispute Settlement Body. Only if a member state formally lodges a complaint can the dispute settlement process be initiated.

Members can bring three kinds of complaints to the DSM, which are highlighted in Article XXIII of GATT 1994, and elaborated on in the Annex on Dispute Settlement. First, if there is a breach of rules by any one member, which is brought to the attention of the DSB by another member, there is a *prima facie* case for a 'nullification and impairment' of the benefits that were meant to accrue for the aggrieved party. There are numerous examples of such cases that allege rule violation. Bernard Hoekman and Michel Kostecki point out that the largest share of cases involves allegations that the principles of non-discrimination have been violated. Second, a member can also advance a 'non-violation' complaint. This means that a member can file a complaint if it considers that any benefit of an agreement under the WTO is being nullified or impaired 'as a result of the application by a Member of any measure, whether or not it conflicts with the provisions of that Agreement'. The third kind of complaint is a 'situation' complaint. Under this provision, even if the complaint does not fit into the first two categories, if the member feels that its gains from a WTO agreement are being undermined by 'any other situation', it can file a complaint against the offending country. All these different provisions point to a legal system that goes beyond the narrow interpretation of the letter of the law and instead encompasses the spirit of the WTO agreements. If consultations between the disputants do not yield results in 60 days, complaints in any of the three categories automatically trigger the establishment of the panel and subsequent stages. If the respondent fails to comply with the recommendations of the DSB, retaliation can be authorized.

Retaliation involves raising duties against the respondent, with variations on the subjects to be covered that depend on the peculiarities of each case and the parties involved. For instance, in the dispute on the EU bananas regime (Ecuador, Guatemala, Honduras, Mexico, and the US versus the EU, wherein the complainants contested the import quotas that the EU allocated for the African Caribbean and Pacific – ACP – group of countries; the panel ruled in favour of the complainants), the provisions for retaliation granted to the US included the 'carousel approach'. As per this approach, retaliatory tariffs of 100% were imposed on a different set of EU exports in every six-month period, thereby hurting the EU in a diversity of sectors. The same dispute also became the first, and therefore landmark, case in which cross-retaliaton was authorized. Having won the case, Ecuador had pointed out that its imports from the EU were too small to allow full retaliation (which had been set at $200 million). Instead, it sought and won the right to cross-retaliate by suspending its concessions under other agreements, including TRIPs. It is worth noting that compensation payments are usually not included as part of the redress mechanism. This reluctance to include compensation payments derives partly from GATT precedent, where, except for one case in 1981 (wherein New Zealand issued a refund to Finland), compensation payments were not accepted. The only case in which compensation has been accepted in the WTO was between the US and Australia in 2000, wherein the beneficiary of an illegal export subsidy was required to reimburse the funds.

All these developments indicate a considerable transformation of the dispute settlement system from its GATT days. In tandem with its increased legal component, however, the DSU has managed to retain the political basis of the agreement. It is the members themselves who nominate potential panellists whose names are put onto the roster, and the approval of the disputants is required on the composition of each dispute settlement panel. And even though the responsibility of settling legal issues lies with the appointed panels, the ultimate dispute settlement body is the DSB, which is constituted by the entire membership of the WTO. Admittedly, in practice, it is almost impossible for the DSB to reject a Panel or Appellate Body decision, given the requirement of negative consensus. But the retention of this political authorization, however perfunctory it might appear, is important, and provides an important insight into the difficult balance that the WTO attempts to tread between the political and the legal. We explore the resulting contradictions in our next section.

The politics of legalization

Legalization, in principle, epitomizes a rules-based trading system. But the impact of this legalization on outcomes is impossible to determine without taking two factors into account: the institutional context within which legalization takes place, and the political processes that give it substance and direction.

While the preceding section illustrated the automatic and binding character of WTO rules, which are enforced via the long arm of its law, this legality sits uncomfortably against the informal rule-making processes that were discussed in Chapter 3. The DSU treats decisions, arrived at through arbitrary processes, as legally binding and can enforce the resulting agreements with stringency. This incongruity, between its powerful legal system of rules and the poorly institutionalized decision-making processes that actually go into the making of that system is a serious one. Its biggest cost is for developing countries, which find themselves legally bound to a system of rules that is not one of their making, but one that they must nonetheless abide by or risk retaliation.

The costs of legalization are rendered doubly high because of the reach of the WTO. In Chapter 4, we analysed the controversial extension of the mandate of the WTO into areas of regulation that take it well inside the state borders and areas that have traditionally fallen within domestic jurisdiction. Legalization means that countries must adhere to contested WTO rules, sometimes even when this entails changing domestic laws. The case that we had discussed as an example of the *de facto* expansion in the WTO's mandate was the US/EU dispute on beef hormones. The WTO's ruling in favour of the US and against the EU ban on the import of hormone-treated beef was seen, in many sectors, as the intrusion of WTO law into the cultural traditions and basic food habits of peoples. Another similar case was the shrimp-turtles dispute, which was brought to the DSB by India, Malaysia, Pakistan, and Thailand in 1997 against the US. In response to domestic concern about the preservation of turtles – an endangered species – and pressure from the fishing industry regarding protection from unfair competition, the US prohibited the shrimp imports from countries that did not use turtle exclusion devices in their shrimp nets. The US defended its import ban by invoking Article XXg of the GATT, which allows trade-restrictive measures for the 'conservation of exhaustible natural resources'. The Panel ruled against the US by focusing on the requirement by Article XX that the measure must not constitute a 'disguised restriction on trade'. But the Appellate Body reversed the ruling on the grounds that the US ban was covered by Article XXg, even though it agreed with the Panel that the ban had resulted in unjustifiable discrimination (as the US had not given the targeted countries adequate time to comply with its requirements). Despite the reprimand to the US, the ruling attracted considerable controversy. It was seen as yet another instance of how some countries could impose their national norms on other members. Further, the case was seen as setting a dangerous precedent that would allow countries to apply even those production process standards that did not affect the physical characteristics of the product, going considerably beyond what was allowed under WTO rules.

The issue of precedent and the expansion of WTO law take us into the second set of problems with the DSU, namely the process of legalization itself. International trade lawyer John Jackson points out that in international law, *stare decisis*, or the common law concept of precedent, does not apply. In practice, however, reference to precedent was frequently used in the dispute settlement process in the GATT, including the formal dispute settlement panel findings. The same remains true of the DSU under the WTO, and in fact permeates even other aspects of institutional process such as decision-making procedures. Rulings become part of the 'practice' – if not formal precedent – under the agreement and influence subsequent decisions of the panels and the Appellate Body. Gregory Shaffer thus writes, 'Individual WTO cases involve more than the judicial resolution of an individual dispute. WTO panel and Appellate Body decisions also produce systemic effects for future cases.' This becomes a problem when developing countries are involved. Those governments that are active participants in the DSM can effectively shape WTO law to their advantage. Such governments are seldom from developing countries, as illustrated in the next section.

In addition to the above, the *de facto* tendency of the Appellate Body to engage in far-reaching interpretation, precedent-creation, and jurisprudence is also problematic. Aspects of contested issues on which negotiations have proven difficult have been brought to the DSB for adjudication. Once the DSB has made a pronouncement on such an area, contested rules that had never been agreed upon manage to make a legal, backdoor entry into the WTO. Given the intrusive scope of WTO rules, it is particularly important that they are carefully negotiated, and countries are fully aware of what they are signing up to and its implications. By effectively substituting negotiation with adjudication, the WTO runs the risk of undermining the legitimacy and longer-term sustainability of its agreements.

Developing countries in the dispute settlement process

At face value, despite the problems highlighted in the previous section, the dispute settlement system seems to have been a success. Hoekman and Kostecki, for instance, point out that over 160 requests were brought to the WTO from 1995 to 2000, which amounted to three times more on a per annum basis than under the GATT. The involvement of developing countries also recorded an increase: over 30% of all the cases involved developing countries as complainants or defendants. Most cases, moreover, tend to produce compliance; the actual use of retaliation has been necessary in only two cases to date. The successes of the dispute settlement system are further borne out in not just the cases that are brought to the panel, but also cases that are settled in the consultation phase. It could be argued that consultation under 'the shadow of law' pre-empts countries from escalating disputes to a point when they can only be resolved through the establishment of a panel.

A closer look at the numbers reveals a less optimistic picture. In a seminal study, Eric Reinhardt and Marc Busch find that developing countries 'are one-third less likely to file complaints against developed states under the WTO than they were under the post-1989 GATT regime'. In contrast, the likelihood of a developing country being the target of a complaint has increased fivefold. Shaffer further notes that developing countries made scarce use of the WTO provision that allows countries to register as third parties to disputes. Only Brazil, India, and Mexico were third parties to more than 8 of the first 273 cases of the WTO, whereas the EU had acted as third party 41 times, and the US 32 times, by August 2002. These figures suggest that as far as a proactive involvement in the dispute settlement process is concerned, developing countries stand at the periphery. This marginalization is costly and entails long-term consequences: WTO law, still in a state of evolution, is being shaped by developed countries to their advantage, as developing countries stand watching on the sidelines.

The marginalization of developing countries from the dispute settlement process has several explanations. First, the costs of access to the dispute settlement mechanism are extremely high. Given the extreme technicalities of each case and the tomes of jurisprudence that have accumulated over the years, specialized legal knowledge is essential for effective participation. However, indigenous legal expertise on the WTO is scarce, and the costs of hiring private lawyers are prohibitively high. Shaffer, for instance, records that even for a relatively small case, a law firm cited a fee of £200,000 for representing a developing country until the panel stage. In high-profile cases, such as the Kodak versus Fuji of Japan-Photographic film case, lawyers charged each of their clients a sum of over $10 million. It is difficult, if not impossible, for developing countries to produce comparable financial resources.

Second, when developing countries do get involved in certain cases that are of critical and unavoidable importance to them, they enter the dispute settlement process as 'one-off' players rather than 'repeat' players. These one-off initiatives, Shaffer points out, tend to be financed by industry or developed countries and usually address the particular cases rather than the long-term, systemic interests of the country. Herein also lies a vicious circle: lack of participation on a sustained basis and without an eye on systemic concerns renders the cost of one-off participation even higher, increasing thereby the reluctance of developing countries to bring their grievances to the DSB.

Third, given the member-driven character of the WTO, the onus of presenting a case lies on the members themselves. This is difficult, not only in terms of the costs involved and locking in of resources until a ruling is made, but also the risk that the stronger party might decide to retaliate against the weaker complainant through unilateral punitive actions outside the WTO. Few developing countries can afford to take on such a risk.

Fourth, in those instances wherein developing countries decide to launch a complaint and win, enforcement of the rulings of the WTO relies on trade retaliation rather than monetary compensation. Small, developing economies seldom have the means to enforce compliance through trade sanctions due to their smaller shares in world trade. To take a hypothetical example, assume that weak Country A were to win a case against a Quad Country B, and were allowed to impose higher tariffs on certain sectors of imports from Country B. But such tariffs would scarcely make a dent on Country B's economy, given that the market of Country A constitutes a minuscule share of B's exports. On the other hand, several sectors within Country A might incur large costs, especially if it is the primary supplier of a particular product. Knowledge of the costs of retaliation would make Country A reluctant to file a dispute in the WTO, even if it would be very likely to win; rather, it would prefer to settle the matter outside the institution. This reluctance of the weaker countries is borne out empirically: no LDC has been involved as either a complainant or a defendant in a dispute to date.

As a result of these imbalances within the dispute settlement system, important in terms of individual cases but also because of the long-term implications of particular rulings on WTO jurisprudence, some steps have been taken. An important step is the establishment of the WTO Advisory Centre on WTO law, which has been set up precisely to provide affordable advice to developing countries. In addition to this, several proposals for reform have also been put forward. The agenda for re-examining the dispute settlement process forms part of the Doha Development Agenda – a new round of trade negotiations that is currently underway (discussed in Chapter 6). Reform proposals have shown a divide between developed and developing countries. Developing countries, in general, have called for longer time periods, consultations in the capitals of LDCs to cut costs of travel to Geneva, greater role for the WTO Advisory Centre, and the right of collective retaliation and trade compensation. Developed countries, on the other hand, have shown a preference for shorter time periods, greater public access, stronger surveillance mechanisms, and weaker retaliation processes. These debates, however, have shown little sign of resolution so far. This is partly because there is little agreement in the research or policy communities on what prompts compliance in the first place. While some scholars have emphasized the importance of retaliation or at least the credible threat of retaliation, others have pointed out that compliance with any norms or rules in international institutions is a product of socialization, learning, and reputation. In the meantime, the agenda of the WTO and the reach of its dispute settlement mechanism continue to expand in several inchoate directions.

Chapter 6
The Doha Development Agenda

The previous chapters highlighted some of the controversies that have dogged the WTO since its inception, and others that have developed as the WTO itself evolves. Amidst these controversies, the first round of multilateral trade negotiations (MTN) under the auspices of the WTO – known as the Doha Development Agenda (DDA) – was launched in November 2001. At this stage, it is difficult to predict exactly how this round will conclude, but two things are certain. First, around the successful conclusion of the round hang not just the interests of particular countries but the very credibility of the WTO as an international organization. The rumblings of discontent targeted at the GATT have grown to a crescendo in the first decade of the WTO, the Uruguay Round is seen to have failed developing countries, and two of the five ministerial meetings of the WTO have come crashing down in failure. Disillusionment with the organization is very high; countries have begun to resort to a plethora of bilateral and regional agreements that threaten any meaningful existence of the WTO and often also further undermine the position of the weak. The Doha *Development* Agenda, as its name indicates, is at least as much an attempt to correct the problems that developing countries and their peoples have encountered as it is an effort to expand the coverage of the agreements. This time, given the history of disappointment and disenfranchisement that comes with it, the WTO cannot afford to fail. Second, the scheduled deadline for the completion of the DDA of January 2005 has proven remarkably ambitious and unrealistic;

all negotiators, politicians and analysts today recognize that negotiations will be more complex, arduous and protracted than they had anticipated. In this chapter, I explore the launching of the DDA (including a brief overview of the failed Seattle Ministerial where the attempt to launch the new round was first made). I review the content and progress of the DDA so far, which offer us some important insights into the new dynamics of WTO negotiations.

The false start to a new round: Seattle Ministerial, 1999

Though the DDA was launched at the fourth ministerial conference of the WTO at Doha in November 2001, the very foundations of the DDA lay in a history of acrimony that was fully borne out in the failed Seattle Ministerial Conference of November 1999. Negotiators had hoped to launch a new development-friendly trade round at Seattle, but the conference itself had ended in a dramatic debacle amidst demonstrations by Non-Governmental Organizations (NGOs). Demonstrators – most non-violent, some anarchist – turned up in the thousands (estimates vary from 30,000 to 60,000) on the streets of Seattle to protest against the WTO. This scale of public outrage came as some surprise for international bureaucrats and negotiators, not least because the abstruse and technical content of trade negotiations had traditionally shielded the GATT and its successor from direct public scrutiny. The perceived democratic deficit of the WTO underlay this outrage; I explore the sources of the perceived democratic deficit of the WTO in the next chapter.

While certain stakeholders in the WTO process tend to view the failure of the Seattle Ministerial as a direct result of the power of NGOs, it is extremely doubtful if a new round could have been launched even if no popular discontent had been expressed. In the run-up to the meeting, the central preoccupation of all members had been the selection of a new Director General to succeed Renato

10. The battle of Seattle, 1999

Ruggiero, which took time and effort away from the necessary preparations for Seattle. Disagreements among the member countries over the launch of the Millennium Round were many and bitter. The push for the launch of a new round came primarily from developed countries who believed that new gains were to be made by expanding the agenda of the WTO beyond the mandate of the existing agreements. The EU had been pushing for the inclusion of the Singapore issues since 1996 (recall that the Singapore issues encompassed competition policy, investment, transparency in government procurement and trade facilitation). The US and Canada had wanted to improve transparency in the Dispute Settlement Mechanism; the US under the Clinton administration also introduced a last-minute proposal at the Seattle conference that a working party on trade and labour be created in the WTO.

Developing countries baulked at almost all the proposals put forth by the developed countries. The issue of labour standard had been acrimoniously debated at the Singapore Ministerial in 1996, with the agreement that matters relating to this controversial issue would be addressed by the International Labour Organization and not the WTO. The US decision to re-open the matter at Seattle was seen as a slap in the face of developing countries. The position of developing countries was simple: until the so-called 'implementation issues' were addressed, there could be no discussion of a new round. Implementation issues referred to the undelivered promises of Uruguay Round and the huge, unanticipated costs of implementing the commitments that they had taken on as part of the agreement. Each party adhered firmly to its position at the Seattle Ministerial and refused to engage in any compromise.

Opaque procedures of functioning, discussed in Chapter 3, further exacerbated antagonisms. Statements by the Chair reinforced developed-developing country differences and did little to enhance the democratic underpinnings of the WTO. For instance, US Trade Representative, Charlene Barshefsky, stated openly that if the process did not reach a consensus text, 'I fully reserve the right to use a more exclusive process to achieve a final outcome. There is no question about either my right as the chair to do it or my intention as the chair to do it.' Developing countries rose back in anger; the meeting ended in failure.

The Doha Development Agenda: Doha Ministerial, 2001

Few of these priorities had changed as the Doha Ministerial approached. Nevertheless, the decision to launch the Doha Development Agenda was arrived at the Doha Ministerial Conference in November 2001. Consensus on the same subject that had proved so problematic only two years ago was a product of three factors. First, partly in response to the debacle at Seattle, and especially as a reaction to the tragic events of 9/11, many countries were coming around to the view that a major gesture was needed to preserve the last vestiges of multilateral cooperation. Second, in the aftermath of Seattle, a conscious attempt had been made to improve at least some of the decision-making processes leading up to the

Ministerial Conference, some of which were discussed in Chapter 3. The WTO also began to improve its external transparency with improved information availability for NGOs. But third, many of the coalitions of developing countries broke ranks in the endgame at Doha as their member countries were bought off through various bilateral deals. Aileen Kwa provides an interesting account of the various carrots and sticks that were used in the run-up to Doha and at the ministerial itself to break the opposition of developing countries. The box below focuses specifically on one specific coalition – the Like-Minded Group – and how the coalition was 'won over' to the 'compromise' at Doha.

The Like-Minded Group of developing countries

The LMG was formed in 1996 and originally comprised Cuba, Egypt, India, Indonesia, Malaysia, Pakistan, Tanzania, and Uganda. By the time of the Doha Ministerial, it had expanded to 14 members. It maintained a vehement opposition to any new negotiations in the WTO until the implementation issues were addressed, and presented detailed, technical papers on several specific issues. The group offered few concessions to the developed world in return.

Recognizing the very high costs of giving in to the demands of the LMG, the Quad began to offer concessions that were targeted towards specific countries within the coalition. Some responded. The African countries accepted the TRIPs and public health declaration and a WTO waiver for the African Caribbean Pacific (ACP) group with the EC. In return, they dropped their opposition to negotiations over industrial tariffs, the environment, and Singapore issues. Promises of assistance for capacity-building and development aid packages were important for the weakest members of the group.

The Egyptians were offered an aid package, while Pakistan was offered both a US aid package and increased EC textile quotas.

Simultaneously, various sticks were brandished. Developing countries were told that the ACP waiver and the TRIPs and public health declaration would be withdrawn. Smaller countries were warned that their preferences would be withdrawn. Ministers were told to either recall recalcitrant ambassadors or ensure that the ambassador softened his position. After Doha, three ambassadors from the LMG are alleged to have been recalled from Geneva because of their hard line.

Once the process of fragmentation had begun, it generated a domino effect. One LMG ambassador explained: 'Once it became evident to the other countries that some were falling off, then they had to consider if it was politically prudent for them to take up a stance of resistance.' On 14 November 2001, India stood alone at the vanguard of resistance; the Doha Development Agenda was launched.

Source: Amrita Narlikar and John Odell, 'The Strict Distributive Strategy for a Bargaining Coalition: The Like Minded Group and the World Trade Organization', forthcoming in John Odell (ed.), *Negotiating Trade: Developing Countries in the WTO and NAFTA*, Cambridge, Cambridge University Press, 2006.

Although a new round of trade negotiations was effectively launched at Doha in spite of the opposition of developing countries, the active participation of developing countries was not entirely in vain. Perhaps the biggest indicator of a newfound sensitivity in the WTO to development concerns is the fact that the new round was given the name of the 'Doha Development Agenda'. Paragraph 2 of the main Ministerial Declaration states: 'The majority of WTO members are developing countries. We seek to place their needs and interests at the heart of the Work Programme adopted in this Declaration.' Arvind Panagariya notes that the main Ministerial Declaration itself uses the expressions 'least developed' countries 29 times, 'developing' countries 24 times, and 'LDC' 19 times, while many of the annexes deal with issues of specific concern to developing countries. It is also important to emphasize that the Doha Development Agenda is little more than a framework on future negotiations. What goes into the actual negotiations and eventual agreements is still up for grabs.

Among the victories for the developing countries, the most widely cited one soon after the Doha Ministerial Conference was the Declaration on Trade Related Intellectual Property Rights (TRIPs) and Public Health. The context for this was the campaign by many developing countries to get cheaper access to expensive, patented drugs used in the treatment of HIV/AIDS (see box below). In language that conforms largely with the proposals of developing countries, particularly as advanced by the coalition on TRIPs and public health. The declaration states: 'the TRIPs agreement does not and should not prevent Members from taking measures to protect public health. . . . In this connection, we reaffirm the right of WTO Members to use, to the full, the provisions in the TRIPs Agreement, which provide flexibility for this purpose.' It is true that the Declaration is really a political one, but its importance goes well beyond the symbolic. The Declaration will make it politically very difficult to bring a dispute against a country that uses compulsory licensing or parallel imports of patented medicines in response to public health emergencies. Member governments will have considerable leeway in determining what constitutes a national emergency. Further, for LDCs, the declaration extends the transition period by another ten years, i.e. upto 2016, on pharmaceutical products.

The AIDS pandemic and TRIPs

Before the advent of the TRIPs agreement, many developing countries had offered minimal patent protection for pharmaceuticals to ensure the provision of cheap medicines for their populations. This changed under TRIPs, which not only required developing countries to provide patent protection, but also restricted the conditions under which compulsory licences could be issued (that is licences to endow another party with the right to produce a product without the patent-holder's permission, intended to produce more affordable generic drugs). Compulsory licences could be issued in instances of national emergency, but even then generic drugs could only be produced for domestic markets and not export.

Faced with the AIDS panedemic, South Africa enacted a Medicines Act in December 1997, which allowed compulsory licensing for the manufacture of generic HIV/AIDS drugs. It also permitted parallel imports so that South Africa could import the cheapest patented medicines.

Pharmaceutical companies in South Africa retaliated with legal action in Pretoria High Court. They argued that the Medicines Act violated constitutional guarantees of property rights, as well as TRIPs, by allowing for uncompensated compulsory licensing. The US backed the pharmaceuticals by placing South Africa on the 'watch list' under Section 301 and suspending duty-free access to its South African imports under the Generalized System of Preferences. Similar pressure was exercised on Brazil and Thailand, which had also used the emergency provisions of TRIPs to issue compulsory licences to address their AIDS crises.

These heavy-handed tactics by the pharmaceuticals and the US catalysed a coalition of developing countries and NGOs into action. The coalition drew a direct link between corporate greed and countless preventable HIV/AIDS-related deaths. It further pointed out that the US was trying to prevent countries from using the emergency exception that TRIPs provided to save lives. Led by the African Group, developing countries and NGOs sought a ministerial declaration that clarified TRIPs provisions on public health, and guaranteed the right of governments to put public health and welfare before patents protection. It was through the efforts of this coalition of state and non-state actors that the Declaration of TRIPs and Public Health was finally agreed upon at the Doha Ministerial.

Source: John Odell and Susan Sell, 'Reframing the Issue, the Coalition on Intellectual Property and Public Health, 2001', forthcoming in John Odell ed., *Negotiating Trade: Developing Countries in the WTO and NAFTA*, Cambridge, Cambridge University Press, 2006.

Besides the Declaration on TRIPs and Public Health, developing countries were promised improved market access in non-agricultural products. In agriculture, the Declaration agreed to special and differential treatment for developing countries in order to ensure that their development needs, including food security and rural development, are met. Implementation-related issues find mention in the main Declaration as well as an independent decision. Two new working groups were set up in areas specifically of interest to developing countries, namely the Working Group on Trade, Debt and Finance and the Working Group on Trade and Transfer of Technology. There was also a focus on enhancing technical assistance and capacity-building in developing countries. Special attention was paid to the needs of the Least Developed Countries (LDCs) as well as the small and vulnerable economies. Seen by many as one of the biggest concessions by the US, the

Declaration sets the agenda for clarifying and improving disciplines of anti-dumping duties, besides subsidies and countervailing measures. And in contrast to the Clinton administration's last minute attempt to put labour standards onto the negotiating table at Seattle, the main Declaration only reaffirmed the decision reached at the Singapore Ministerial. Paragraph 44 of the main declaration affirms that the provisions of Special and Differential Treatment (S&D) 'form an integral part of the WTO Agreements.' These are no small achievements, but at what cost were they obtained?

In return for the above gains, developing countries paid a potentially heavy price. Although they had raised the demand that the implementation issues be addressed before the launch of a new round, they have been linked to the negotiating process of the new round and in exchange for new commitments. This means that developing countries will pay twice over for their so-called gains from the Uruguay Round – precisely the outcome that the LMG had sought to avoid. Through ambiguous language and some deft negotiations in the last minute, the Singapore issues were introduced into the DDA. The problems with the process whereby the Singapore issues were introduced were discussed in Chapter 3; the same ambiguous phrasing and disputed process was to contribute to the confrontation at the Cancun Ministerial Conference in 2003. In areas that have been explicitly devoted to the interests of developing countries, such as technical assistance, technology transfer, and the new work programme for small economies, there is little by way of concrete deliverables. In the absence of any clear provisions on where the funding for these capacity-building and technology transfer activities will come from, there is a real danger that these clauses will remain little more than an expression of good will.

In many ways, the naming of the new round as the Doha Development Agenda suggests an attempt by all parties to restore the faith of the marginalized developing countries in the WTO.

However, the process whereby the DDA was actually agreed upon has meant that this faith remains tenuous. Even though the preparatory process leading up to the Doha Ministerial Conference allowed for greater internal transparency and inclusion of developing countries, many developing countries complained in confidential interviews with the author that these good practices were thrown out of the window when the crunch came at Doha. India and Pakistan, for instance, had protested vehemently when Stuart Harbinson issued the Chair's text under his own authority, but this text was nonetheless used as the basis of the negotiation. Stories of bilateral pressure that was exercised on the capitals abound. Similarly, there are several anecdotes of how 'difficult' ambassadors were brought under pressure (e.g. one ambassador was allegedly asked, 'Do you want to be consulted or do you want to be insulted?'). Consensus on the DDA, reached under such circumstances, would come to haunt the negotiation process most visibly at the next ministerial at Cancun.

Collapse at Cancun

Trade negotiators met at the biennial WTO ministerial meeting – in September 2003 in Cancun – to go about the task of completing the negotiations for the DDA to try and meet the deadline of January 2005. They had spent the previous two years in preparation for the Cancun Ministerial under the auspices of the Trade Negotiations Committee (TNC) set up by the Doha Declaration. The TNC established seven negotiating bodies – agriculture, non-agricultural market access (NAMA), services, rules, trade and environment, geographical indications for wines and spirits, and reform of the Dispute Settlement Understanding – to conduct negotiations in each of the specific areas. Organization and streamlining of the process of negotiation, however, could not overcome the deep political differences that existed among countries over the issues under discussion, and the Ministerial ended in failure.

The year 2002 was dotted with missed deadlines and only a few achievements. The major success story of the year was an agreement within the TRIPs Council on parallel imports of essential medicines by countries lacking indigenous capacity for production. As a result of this agreement, developing countries can now import cheap generic drugs produced under compulsory licensing in other developing countries. The subsequent preparatory process was swamped by attempts to reach agreement on the extremely nettling issue of agriculture, and differences continued across issues. As the date for the Cancun Ministerial approached, the Chair of the General Council – Ambassador Carlos Perez del Castillo – attempted to break the deadlock by issuing a compromise Chair's text under his own authority. The reactions that this text provoked from developing countries were discussed in Chapter 3; the joint EU-US text on agriculture (August 13) did little to alleviate the misgivings of developing countries that the two giants would 'pull another Blair House Accord on us'. (The Blair House Accord provided the basis for the Agreement on Agriculture in the Uruguay Round, which was reached between the EU and the US and at the exclusion of developing countries.) The Cancun Ministerial thus began on a note of distrust from developing countries – distrust that the Doha Ministerial had itself exacerbated – which soon developed into a full-scale North-South confrontation.

Problems in the consultation and decision-making processes at Cancun and their role in exacerbating the tension between developed and developing countries were discussed in Chapter 3. The substance of the discussions on three issue-areas has also proven highly problematic. The biggest sources of impasse at Cancun were agriculture, Singapore issues, and cotton. Before discussing these three issues, however, one caveat is in order: the focus on the three issues does not imply that any of the other issues were resolved or will provide any easy solutions in the future. Differences over issues such as NAMA and S & D continued to simmer at Cancun, and will re-emerge in the forthcoming talks.

Agriculture had proven to be the knottiest of issues for the summer of 2003 and became the bête noir of Cancun. Until the EU and the US came out with their joint draft in August, the Cairns Group countries with an offensive interest in large-scale agricultural liberalization had hoped that the US would back their position. Similarly, countries with a more defensive interest in agriculture had hoped that the EU would support their position. Developing countries from both sets of interests came together under the leadership of Brazil and India when they realized that the EU and the US had joined forces to produce a highly unsatisfactory text. Herein lay the origins of one of the most interesting coalitions of developing countries in recent times – the G20 – which had as its core membership such emerging powers as Brazil, China, India, South Africa, and Argentina.

The G20 put forth its draft on 2 September 2003, which was signed by Argentina, Bolivia, Brazil, Chile, China, Colombia, Costa Rica, Cuba, Ecuador, El Salvador, Guatemala, India, Mexico, Pakistan, Paraguay, Peru, the Philippines, South Africa, Thailand and Venezuela. The group proposed more radical cuts on domestic support measures than the EU-US draft had committed, including a capping on the Green Box subsidies. On market access, it overcame potential differences between countries like Brazil with an offensive interest and countries like India with a defensive interest, by demanding greater commitments from developed countries. For instance, the draft stated, 'All developed countries shall provide duty-free access to all tropical products and others mentioned in Preamble to the Agreement on Agriculture as well as to other agricultural products representing [ ]% of exports from developing countries.' It further stated. 'There will be no commitments regarding TRQ expansion and reduction in quota tariff rates for developing countries.' In keeping with the agenda of the G33 (see box), it pressed for a Special Safeguard Mechanism for developing countries. On export subsidies, the G20 proposed the elimination of export subsidies of interest to developing countries within a target date and further a commitment to reduce export subsidies on remaining products by a later specified date. References to Special and Differential Treatment appeared throughout the proposal.

The Chair's revised text, also known as the Derbez text and presented on 13 September, did little to address the concerns of the G20; in some ways it was even seen to go backwards. Amongst other objections to the draft, the G20 pointed out that reductions proposed in domestic support were inadequate, and there was an imbalance in the commitments between developed and developing countries on market access. Interestingly, in contrast to the LMG that had collapsed in the endgame at Doha, the G20 did not collapse under divide and rule tactics at Cancun. Each side stood united at Cancun, and neither backed down on the last day of the conference.

Coalitions at Cancun

Some coalitions at Cancun dated back at least to the Doha Ministerial, if not earlier, while others were a product of new challenges. Besides the G20, three others emerged as key players at Cancun.

The Core Group of developing countries initially comprised 12 members: Bangladesh, Cuba, Egypt, India, Indonesia, Kenya, Malaysia, Nigeria, Pakistan, Venezuela, Zambia, and Zimbabwe. In response to a paper by the EU, which had assumed that the negotiation on Singapore issues would commence after Cancun, the Core Group submitted a joint statement in July pointing out that explicit consensus was a necessary condition for negotiations to consensus. The group continued to operate at the Cancun Ministerial and expanded in its membership.

The Alliance on Strategic Products and Special Safeguard Mechanism initially comprised over 20 countries from Central and Latin America, South Asia, Southeast Asia, and

Africa. The group proposed that developing countries be allowed to designate certain products as 'strategic products' on which they would not be expected to take on any new commitments. A special safeguard mechanism would be established to protect the domestic markets of these countries against import surges. By the 13 September, the group had expanded to 33 members.

The third interesting coalition of Cancun was the G90. The African Group, ACP, and the LDCs came together to coordinate their positions on the final day of the conference, leading to the creation of the G90. While the G90's immediate concern was to resist an inclusion of negotiations on the Singapore issues through the back door, it has been increasingly vocal since Cancun on issues such as S & D, the erosion of preferences, and potential problems from a rapid liberalization of NAMA.

The coalitions of Cancun were striking in their ability to endure pressures and remain united in the endgame at Cancun, but also their durability thereafter. These coalitions presented detailed, well-researched proposals at Cancun and afterwards. They also made a conscious attempt to coordinate their positions. Representatives across coalitions met frequently at the ministerial for joint consultations and new 'alliances of sympathy'. Recognizing that this bloc unity holds the key to their bargaining power, especially in the light of their history of failed experiments with issue-based coalitions, the coalitions of Cancun have attempted to retain their intra- and inter-group cohesion in its aftermath.

Source: Amrita Narlikar and Diana Tussie, 'The G20 at the Cancun Ministerial: Developing Countries and Their Evolving Coalitions', *World Economy*, July 2004; and Amrita Narlikar, *International Trade and Developing Countries: Bargaining Coalitions in the GATT and WTO* (London: Routledge, 2003)

The Singapore issues provided another terrain for a North-South showdown. Making expected use of the ambiguity of the language of 'explicit consensus' that had been introduced in the Doha Declaration, the EU's interpretation was that the Singapore issues were already within the DDA mandate and all that countries had to do in Cancun was to negotiate modalities. Developing countries, in contrast, operating as the Core Group on Singapore issues, were vehement in their insistence that 'Explicit consensus on the modalities is required for negotiations to commence not consensus on how to classify and group the different procedural and structural aspects of the Singapore issues.' This difference in interpretation led to considerable acrimony, first over the Castillo draft and subsequently over the Derbez draft. The latter text, meant to be a compromise text, catalysed the anger of many developing countries as it outlined the modalities for government procurement and trade facilitation and stated that 'we decide to commence negotiations' in the two areas. On investment too, the text allowed for a period of clarification, but then went on to state that modalities would have to be agreed upon by a specified date (that were still to be discussed). Only in the area of competition policy was the wording less rigorous, leaving this area primarily to the clarification stage and with no immediate binding commitments. But this was cold comfort to developing countries, which had opposed the inclusion of the Singapore issues in the first place and had believed that the 'explicit consensus' requirement would prevent any last-minute backdoor inclusions. In spite of differences among developing countries (some argued that the Singapore issues could be 'unbundled' and discussed individually on their own merit, while others advanced the position that the Singapore issues represented a different genre of issues and should be treated as one basket), they were united in their opposition to the Derbez text.

On the final day of the Cancun meeting, Derbez chose to focus on the Singapore issues – a choice that prompted some surprise from delegations in subsequent interviews with the author, which had expected a focus on agriculture. And here as well lay another deal-breaker. Botswana, speaking on behalf of the Africa Group, declared that they could not accept any deal that included even one of the Singapore issues. Japan and South Korea reacted by announcing that any deal would have to include all four of the Singapore issues. The intractability of the Singapore issues finally led Derbez to throw in the towel.

While the Singapore issues provided the immediate cause for the collapse at Cancun, differences over the Cotton Initiative had contributed to the crisis of faith in the WTO. Four West and Central African countries had proposed a complete phase-out of cotton subsidies in the developed countries, and financial compensation until the phase-out was complete. The US position, however, was to refuse to discuss cotton subsidies and instead have a broader discussion on textiles and clothing. Even after all the deliberations on cotton under the chairmanship of Supachai, the Derbez text leaned dangerously close to the US position. It called for consultations to 'address the impact of distortions that exist in the trade of cotton, man-made fibres, textiles and clothing to ensure comprehensive consideration of the entirety of the sector'. It committed no new resources towards financial compensation, and instead only instructed some of the international organizations to direct existing programs and resources to economic diversification in countries where cotton accounted for a major share in GDP. The disappointment and shock of the African countries to this proposal was considerable, and was echoed by other countries as well. The meanness of concessions on an area that constitutes such a small fraction of the economy and populations of developed countries was seen as symbolic of the refusal of developed countries to make any concessions at all for even the poorest of the world's poor. The cotton issue may have been a small one in economic terms, but it contributed to the growing levels of distrust and antagonism.

The closure of the conference occurred on an acerbic note of finger-pointing and name-calling. US Trade Representative Robert Zoellick assigned blame to the 'won't do' countries at Cancun, and announced that the US would not wait for these countries and instead seek bilateral agreements outside of the WTO. EU Trade Commissioner Pascal Lamy reiterated that the WTO was a 'medieval organization'. That the last two of the three WTO ministerials had failed did not augur well for the future of the organization. At Cancun itself, outside the corridors and the meeting rooms, NGOs claimed victory for the poor of the world.

A jubilant reinterpretation of the Beatles by NGOs in the aftermath of the collapse at the Cancun Ministerial

Our world is not for sale, my friend
Just to keep you satisfied.
You say you'll bring us health and wealth
Well we know that you just lied.
We don't care too much for Zoellick
Zoellick can't buy the world.
Can't buy the wo-orld, listen while we tell you so
Can't buy the wo-orld, no no nooo!
No new issues in Cancun
You know that's just not right.
No arm-twisting delegates
Or Green Rooms through the night.
We don't care too much for bullies
Business can't rule the world.
Can't rule the wo-orld, listen while we tell you so
Can't rule the wo-orld no no nooo!~!

11. **Demonstration by the Trade Justice Movement, Trafalgar Square, 3 November 2001**

The show must go on: DDA after Cancun

Despite the triumphalism in the press of some developing countries and NGO publications, and the recurrent adage of 'No deal is better than this deal', all the players recognized that the situation of impasse represented victory for no one. After a temporary lull, the negotiators were finally able to break the stalemate in the celebrated 'July Package' on 31 July 2004. Two factors allowed the negotiators to overcome the impasse that had proved so difficult to resolve at Cancun.

First, the developed countries had come to recognize the altered nature of the game as a result of the change in the participation of developing countries. In the past, coalitions of developing countries had adopted some extremely intransigent positions through the greater part of the negotiation, and then fragmented in the endgame in response to bilateral deals. This record led developed countries to assume that the same pattern would be repeated in Cancun, and hence that no concessions made collectively to the counter-coalitions of the G20, ACP, G33, LDCs, and others would be necessary. The fact that the coalitions of Cancun stood united in the face of such pressures demonstrated to the developed countries that they would have to make at least some concessions if a complete breakdown in the Doha talks was to be avoided. Second, both sides recognized that the WTO could not afford another failure without a serious blow to its credibility and its very existence. The deadline for agreeing to a framework package for the negotiations, which had evaded Cancun, had been re-set for the end of July and had to be met.

The July Package – a framework where all the details have yet to be negotiated – postpones the deadline for the completion of the Doha Round to an unspecified date and thereby presents a reality check on the ambitions of the Doha Ministerial. As a compromise from the EU, all the Singapore issues except trade facilitation have been dropped. Even on trade facilitation, in response to the concerns of developing countries, the Framework provides that developing countries will not be required to implement the final agreement where they lack the necessary capacity or infrastructure. Cotton has been placed on a separate fast-track, in contrast to the US position at Cancun that had attempted to scuttle cotton within a broader sector. But the annex on agriculture presents the icing on the cake.

The annex on agriculture presents a 'tiered' formula approach for the phasing out of domestic subsidies. This means that countries with more domestic support will have to make greater reductions, while developing countries will be allowed longer implementation periods as well as lower reduction coefficients. The annex states that direct and indirect export subsidies will be phased out, and the tiered formula will ensure that market access commitments of developed and developing countries will not be the same. Both developed and developing countries will be able to designate sensitive products on which smaller tariff cuts will be required. In addition, developing countries will be allowed to designate Special Products, which will take into account their non-trade concerns of food security, rural development, and so forth. The Special Safeguard Mechanism has also been incorporated. LDCs will not be required to reduce tariffs. Developed countries have also promised to make a 'down payment' in the form of a 20% cut in their subsidies in the first year. Given the extent of differences at Cancun between the G20 and G33 on one side, and the EU and the US on the other, the annex on agriculture is no mean achievement, and gestures like the down payment may help restore the low levels of trust that came to the fore at Cancun.

A closer inspection, however, reveals some critical actual and potential loop-holes. The 20% reduction in subsidies as down payment is to be calculated against bound levels rather than applied levels; as developed countries, in practice, subsidize well below the bound levels, this may result in minimal real reductions. Market access may well be rendered meaningless depending on what developed countries decide to include on their list of sensitive products. Even though developed countries have agreed to a phase-out of domestic subsidies, Green Box subsidies will still be allowed and could be manipulated through reclassification and redefinitions. Similarly, much will depend on how the tiered formula actually evolves, and what dates are negotiated for export subsidy reductions.

Besides dangers that even the July Package might eventually result in only limited agricultural liberalization, non-agricultural market access remains a Pandora's Box on which little progress was made in July. This was largely because of the developing country position that they would not negotiate on this issue as long as the deadlock on agriculture persisted. Already, potential rifts are evident here, many of which are actually within the developing world. For instance, the first draft of the July package stated that the reduction commitments of developing countries in agriculture and the non-agricultural sector would take into account 'their levels of development in particular sectors'. This provision, however, was watered down as it was seen as privileging some of the smaller economies against the middle-income economies of the developing world. The language of 'shall be taken into account' was changed to 'should', and an MFN provision was thrown in to guard against preferential treatment along these lines. It is extremely likely that these differences will re-surface once the actual negotiations under this framework begin.

By the time of the July Package and thereafter, moreover, even though some of the older issues like agriculture have shown signs of resolution, new problems have emerged. For instance, with the end of the Agreement on Textiles and Clothing – something that developing countries had long desired – there is now a sense of considerable alarm that many developing countries will lose their markets to the highly competitive textile exports from China. Similarly, as the pace of liberalization increases, certain groups of countries like the ACP group are concerned about their declining preferences in specific regional markets. The July Package, moreover, has also thrown up some critical process-related concerns. The July Package was largely a deal struck by 'Five Interested Parties', that is, Australia, Brazil, EU, India, and the US. Admittedly, Brazil and India maintained close links with other developing countries, particularly via the G20. But several other countries that were not a part of the G20 complained of marginalization from the process.

All the above problems indicate a trend towards increasing differences within the developing world, which is likely to continue as the nitty-gritty of the negotiations takes shape and they have to engage in specific give and take rather than grand posturing over principles. Cancun will be presented as an exemplar of the successful coalition diplomacy of developing countries, when developing countries were finally able to put up a united front and refuse to accept a sub-optimal agreement. But it remains to be seen if the coalitions of Cancun are able to withstand the pressures of increasing differentiation within and pressures from without as the negotiations progress.

Finally, to return our focus on the big picture: what do the failures of Seattle and Cancun versus the 'successes' of Doha and the July Package tell us about the health of the WTO as an international organization? Could institutional reform within the WTO help in establishing institutional equilibrium, which might curb the pendulum swings of alternating success and failure? And, if so, then what directions might institutional reform take? I explore these issues in the next and concluding chapter.

Chapter 7
The burden of governance

Over the past five years, the WTO has lurched from one crisis to another. Admittedly no multilateral process, especially when it involves such a diversity of countries, can be expected to be an easy ride. But the failure rate of WTO ministerial conferences and recurring stalemates are considerably higher than the GATT had ever encountered, and seem only to be increasing in frequency. The public protests against the organization, particularly at the Seattle Ministerial and subsequent meetings, suggest a perceived disfranchisement on a scale and intensity that is qualitatively different from the kind reflected in the occasional demonstrations in the 1990s against 'GATTzilla'. These difficulties point to a deeper malaise that afflicts the WTO, rather than just the teething problems of a new organization, and have prompted considerable soul-searching among participants and observers alike.

Recent reflections on the nature of the WTO as an international organization, as well as related proposals for institutional reform, have taken three directions. The first traces recent problems in terms of a 'how' question: the persistence of obsolete methods of decision-making have pushed the organization to this point in crisis. Reforming these processes will put a stop to the recurrence of crises and allow a smoother governance of the international trading system. Others argue that the question is a deeper, more fundamental one – a 'what' question – the problem with the WTO is not how it goes about its business but really what it does or has

12. The democratic deficit of the WTO has entered public debate in a way that it had never done in the years of the GATT

come to do. The third form of scepticism derives primarily from a 'who' question, but one that also relates to the previous two, which is: we need to take a closer look at whom the WTO is really accountable to. According to this last view, the deep-rooted, democratic deficit of the organization holds the key to its recurrent crises. A brief overview of these different strands of thought follows below, as well as the insights that they offer on how the WTO got to this point and ways in which it might evolve.

Reforming a 'medieval' organization

After the failure of the Cancun Ministerial, EU Trade Commissioner, and now the new Director-General Elect, Pascal Lamy's announcement that this 'medieval' organization was in urgent need of reform did not come as news to the disfranchised majority of developing country delegates, who had been protesting against the exclusionary decision-making processes in the WTO for years. But with developed countries turning to the issue of institutional reform, the agenda entered the mainstream debate and turned to the immediate and obvious target of consensus-based decision-making.

Proposals for and against a consultative board

Commenting on the inefficient and arduous decision-making procedures at Seattle and Cancun, some governments and individuals advanced the view that the WTO sets itself up for failure by requiring that all decisions be arrived at through consensus among its 148 members. Previously, in the days of the GATT and the first few years of the WTO, only a few members would be present in the Green Room meetings, allowing consensus to emerge. Improved transparency of the Green Room processes since Seattle has facilitated the participation of members that had traditionally been excluded from decision-making. But with 148 members at the negotiating table, decision-making has becoming inefficient, if not impossible. The only way of overcoming this fatal flaw in the WTO is the establishment of an executive or consultative board of some sort.

Proposals for a consultative board come from several sources. The EU has maintained a consistent support for this view in the aftermath of the failures at Seattle as well as Cancun. Canada put forth the proposal for a new committee resembling the UN Security

Council in regional representation and the rotation of non-permanent members. Mexico proposed the transformation of the Green Room into a 'Glass Room', in which 25% of the WTO's members (34 at the time of the proposal) would participate; the 15 members with the greatest shares in world trade would act as permanent members. The remaining 19 members would be chosen according to regional criteria, where the selection would be made by the countries of the relevant region. Jeffrey Schott and Jayashree Watal made a similar proposal in a research paper in 2000 of an informal steering committee of 20 members based on absolute value of foreign trade and geographic representation ensuring representation with at least two members from each region. In 2003, Richard Blackhurst and David Hartridge argued for a consultative board. The larger countries would have permanent seats on the board, while the other members would be divided into groups with one seat per group (occupied by members within each group on a rotating basis). All these proposals have emphasized that that the board would have only consultative, consensus-building powers and not any decision-making ones.

Most developing countries, including those who have found it difficult to gain access to the small group meetings, have come out strongly against proposals for a consultative board of any kind. From their perspective, the only thing that the WTO has going for it, particularly when compared against the international financial institutions and their system of weighted voting, is its one-member-one-vote consensus-based decision-making processes. The creation of a consultative board that distinguishes between permanent and non-permanent members would destroy whatever semblance of international equality exists in the WTO by effectively creating a system of weighted voting based on world trade shares.

There are three practical reasons as to why a consultative body, created along any of the variations suggested above, would be deeply problematic. First, given the binding nature and intrusive potential of WTO rules, it is unlikely that individual countries would accept the advisory recommendations of any inter-state consultative body. Most members of the WTO have come to recognize from harsh experience that the consultative phase of the negotiations is also the agenda-setting one, and entry into the final decision-making phase is no substitute for participation in the initial consultative phase. Second, non-permanent seats based on regional representation are especially unlikely to work given the vast differences that exist even within regions when it comes to specific issue areas. Third, as one group of developing countries has noted, 'Creation of an advisory board would formalise the exclusion of a large number of Members from the process of consultations.'

A possible way of striking a balance between the efficiency and legitimacy arguments to find a compromise between the one-member-one-vote consensus-based decision-making and the consultative board. Elements of this compromise can be found in a proposal that was put forth by Vinod Rege, Advisor to the Commonwealth developing countries in Geneva. Rege suggests the creation of an Informal Steering Committee at the beginning of each year, on the recommendations of the Chair of the General Council in consultation with the other chairpersons of the three councils. The list of participants would reflect the different stages of development and interests of the member countries, and would depend on the particular schedule of meetings and issues under discussion for that year. The Committee would not be a standing committee but could be invoked when small-group consultations became necessary. The Rege proposal could be extended to the creation of sub-committees with different memberships, depending on the interests of particular countries in specific issue areas based on invitation by the chairs but also self-selection. Two problems, however, stand in the way of implementing such a proposal. First, some developing countries object to a consultative body as a matter of principle and are unlikely to accept any variation of this idea. And second, while the developed Rege variant allows the consultative body flexibility to operate at different sub-committee levels, the complicated manoeuvres required to establish these committees might turn out to be as inefficient as the current consensus-based process.

Diplomatic flexibility versus rules-based certainty

Another question of institutional reform over which daggers have been drawn relates less to any one procedure than to the broader manner of the WTO's functioning. It is interesting to note that countries that are in favour of the consultative body also usually emphasize the continued benefits of GATT-derived negotiating flexibility and diplomatic improvisation as providing the groundwork for the WTO. In contrast, many developing countries that have supported the continuation of one-member-one-vote, consensus-based decision-making have advanced proposals to strengthen rules about the negotiation process.

The like minded group (LMG) has made many formal and informal proposals advancing the latter view. In 2002, for instance, the LMG argued that: 'uncertainty in the process makes it difficult for many Members to prepare themselves for the conferences. Some basic principles and procedures for this Member-driven organization need to be agreed upon, so that both the preparatory process and the conduct of the Ministerial Conference are transparent, inclusive and predictable.' To this end, the group proposed that 'Any negotiating procedure to be adopted should be approved by Members by consensus in formal meetings.' The document insisted that 'The draft ministerial declaration should be based on consensus. Where this is not possible, such differences should be fully and appropriately reflected in the draft ministerial declaration'; and 'A draft ministerial declaration can only be forwarded to the Ministerial Conference by the General Council upon consensus to do so.' The group found support from other developing countries on this matter, including in a proposal put forth by a group of African countries. Some NGOs have taken the proposal for greater formality of rules even further. For instance, ten mainstream NGOs (The Third World Network, Oxfam International, Public Services International, WWF International, The Center for International Environmental Law, Focus on the Global South, The Institute for Agriculture and Trade Policy, The African Trade Network, International Gender and Trade Network, and the Tebtebba International Center for Indigenous Peoples' Rights) stated in a memorandum in July 2003 that 'Meetings should all be official, with minutes taken down and circulated to Members for amendments or confirmation.'

The second view is typified in a proposal put forth jointly by Australia, Canada, Hong Kong, Korea, Mexico, New Zealand, Singapore, and Switzerland in 2002. This proposal makes a direct reference to the LMG draft and presents an alternative view on many of the points presented in the LMG proposal. In contrast to the call for explicit rules and clearly laid down procedures, the eight-country proposal argues that 'Prescriptive and detailed approaches to the preparatory process are inappropriate and will not create the best circumstances for consensus to emerge in the Cancun meeting.' It stresses the importance of flexibility in a member-driven organization. In contrast to the LMG proposal, which suggests a suspicion of ministerial-level processes, this proposal argues that 'The preparatory process should leave space for the Ministerial Conference to take up those issues which call for resolution at the ministerial level.'

The two sets of views have proven difficult to reconcile, not least because they are based on conflicting interests and abilities. The LMG view conforms neatly with Stephen Krasner's argument that developing countries seek authoritative regimes. Their search for greater certainty, and hence more formalized and tighter rules, derives from their comparatively limited capabilities to understand and negotiate the increasing technicality of an expanding set of issues that fall within the mandate of the WTO. Countries with well-identified proactive interests in the WTO and an ability to pursue them, in contrast, stress the virtues of flexibility and attach considerable importance to the diplomacy that has traditionally provided the groundwork for GATT and WTO negotiations. They translate into two competing visions of the WTO as an international organization. The LMG-type view is, on balance, of a limited, technocratic organization with a well-circumscribed mandate and tightly bound by a clearly specified set of rules and procedures. In contrast, the developed country view is one of an expansive organization that cuts across issue areas, and is driven by politics rather than technicalities and detailed rules. It is also one that relies significantly on flexibility of negotiating procedure, small-group meetings within and outside the WTO, and considerable political involvement. These two divergent visions have some important implications for the ways in which the WTO might be held accountable to its various constituencies, as discussed in the last section of this chapter.

Questioning the mandate

The second set of debates about the WTO has focused on its mandate. Scepticism about the reach of the WTO derives from member countries and NGOs.

Among the member countries, discord about the scope of the WTO's evolving mandate is inevitable, and presents a general divide between the developed and developing world. Much of the agenda for an expansion of GATT/WTO rules into new areas has been led by developed countries, for instance the inclusion of services, TRIPs, TRIMs, and subsequently the drive to include the Singapore issues. However, as Chapter 3 argued, many developing countries find it difficult to keep pace even with the existing negotiating agenda and implement current agreements, let alone have the expertise to identify their interests in newer areas. Given these logistical difficulties, the default position of developing countries has been to 'just say no' to the entry of absolutely any new issue into the WTO and reiterate the importance of resolving some of the older problems. The extreme divergence of these views presents the

WTO with a Catch 22 situation. If the WTO slows the pace of the negotiations, it risks losing the commitment of its developed countries; if it continues with the expansion, however, in line with the agenda of the developed countries, it risks the further marginalization of the majority of its members and a further decline in the legitimacy of its decisions.

In an attempt to keep both constituencies aboard, some scholars and policy-makers have proposed the dismantling of the Single Undertaking and its replacement with multiple tracks based on 'variable geometry'. Still in its early stages, this idea has not attracted much reaction yet from developed or developing countries. It is worth recalling that the EU expansion has adopted a similar dual-track mechanism, and seems to be working successfully. If it does enter the policy debate in a serious way in the WTO, however, two caveats are worth bearing in mind. First, the Single Undertaking was crucial to the making of the Grand Bargain that led to the creation of the WTO. It still remains the case that cross-issue exchange of concessions underlies the completion of any deal, and the existence of multiple tracks will make such concessions difficult. Second, by avoiding commitments on areas covered by a hypothetical Track 2 and taking on only Track 1 commitments, developing countries will effectively marginalize themselves from the critical agenda-setting and rule-making phase for Track 2. As countries now seeking accession to the WTO are learning, the costs of late entry can be quite high. Vigilance is especially important in multilateralism when such divergent sets of interests and visions are involved and power inequalities are so extreme.

While developing countries have complained about the fast pace of the negotiations and expanding agenda, many NGOs have expressed dissatisfaction with the WTO for the opposite reason: that its agenda is in fact far too narrow, and thereby privileges trade over all other values. As per this view, a re-balancing of interests within the WTO is necessary, perhaps even through a constitutional mechanism, to ensure that trade interests are balanced by human rights, environment, labour standards, gender and income inequalities within states, development, and so forth. While there is certainly a case to be made for expanding the reach of global norms in these key domains, whether they should be governed through the WTO is highly questionable for four central reasons.

First, as Chapter 4 illustrated, the problem with the WTO seems to be excessive regulation, not an insufficiency thereof, as countries increasingly complain of the shrinking of national policy space. The discontent of populations worldwide over having to adhere to WTO standards (e.g. on GMOs) has been pronounced. Expanding WTO regulations even further into contested non-trade concerns would shrink this national policy space further, depriving states of their rights and ability to adopt goals that conform to the imperatives and priorities of particular societies. States are unlikely to react lightly or warmly to further encroachments into their domestic jurisdictions.

Second, as Chapters 3 and 4 together argued, the expansion in the agenda of the WTO has not been matched by commensurate changes in the everyday workings of the WTO. Expanding the WTO into areas such as human rights and the environment would effectively accord the organization all the functions that a world government might be expected to perform. The WTO is structurally ill equipped to perform these functions with any level of efficiency. Even if the organization were sufficiently reformed to allow it vastly expanded powers and funds to regulate in these areas, it is doubtful if the WTO could do so legitimately. As the next section will illustrate, the bureaucratic accountability with which the WTO operates differs considerably from the vertical accountability that one expects of democratic governments. The WTO is already too big for its boots; to expand it even further into areas where it was never intended to go would be inefficient and injudicious.

Third, despite the stated good intentions of the non-trade agenda, it is difficult in practice to ensure that these noble standards will not be used as non-tariff barriers against imports from the developing countries and deprive them of whatever comparative advantage they enjoy. Standards of human rights, environment, and labour are often closely related to cultural and social detail at the national and sub-national levels; the establishment of universal standards in these areas has, even in principle, been a long-contested issue. Entrusting the WTO with guarding such contested standards through a trade link, which might be exploited for protectionist purposes, is likely to jeopardize the legitimacy of its decisions even further.

Finally, any petitions to expand the WTO into areas such as labour standards and human rights must be set against the charter for the ITO. Recall from Chapter 1 that the Havana Charter was considerably more expansive than the GATT or the WTO, and the fate that it suffered as a stillborn project. By logrolling the many contradictory interests of all its different constituencies, the ITO project collapsed under the weight of its own ambitions. In contrast, the successes of the GATT lay in the self-imposed limitations of its agenda. Increased global integration notwithstanding, what was politically impossible then should be approached at least with high levels of political caution now.

My scepticism about the further expansion of the WTO into explicitly non-trade concerns should not be interpreted as a counsel of despair. An international management of certain minimum standards or norms may be possible by improving the coherence of the global governance system. Parallel mechanisms emerging from the private sector, for instance in the form of norms of corporate social responsibility for multinational corporations, have begun to take shape. Article V of the Agreement establishing the WTO requires the General Council to make appropriate arrangements 'for effective cooperation with other international organizations that have responsibilities related to those of the WTO'. Paragraph 5 of the Main Doha Declaration reinforces this point:

> We are aware that the challenges Members face in a rapidly changing international environment cannot be addressed through

measures taken in the trade field alone. We shall continue to work with the Bretton Woods institutions for greater coherence in global economic policy-making.

Reducing the democratic deficit of the WTO

The third set of responses to the recurrent crises within the WTO refers to the organization's deep-rooted democratic deficit. This deficit is a product of the fact that the millions affected by the rules of the WTO are unable to have any direct influence on the rule-making process. As per this view, problematic decision-making processes among member states, the expansion of the organization's mandate into contested areas, and the incongruities between the weak institutional structure and the legally binding and expansive mandate, only exacerbate the democratic deficit rather than actually cause it.

13. Admittedly, the immediate reaction of the developed world was to blame the intransigence of the developing countries for the failure of the Cancun Ministerial, illustrated in this cartoon. This knee-jerk reaction, however, was fortunately followed by a greater willingness to engage among all parties.

It is certainly true that rule-making in the WTO can appear far removed from the people that it affects. NGOs or any other affected members of civil society have no right of representation in the WTO, whose business is conducted by national delegations from member governments. These delegations in turn are made up of national bureaucrats (often from the ministry of commerce or its equivalent and the foreign ministry) rather than elected representatives of the people. One of the few inputs that voters have into the process is at the time of elections, when they elect representatives to form governments. But it is usually the ministers, with inputs from officials in the relevant ministries, who eventually decide whom to appoint to the delegation in Geneva, which is involved in WTO decision-making. This long chain of delegation means that even in the best of democracies, national delegations in the WTO are distant from their electorates. Given this distance, it is not surprising that many NGOs have called for greater external transparency in WTO negotiations, and even some direct NGO representation in the WTO with observer status if not decision-making powers. Similarly, others have emphasized the importance of greater political participation at the ministerial level as well as inter-parliamentary meetings that bring the decision-making down at least to the level of their elected representatives rather than faceless bureaucrats in Geneva.

On the question of whether increased ministerial or parliamentary involvement would actually improve the WTO accountability to affected stakeholders, the verdict is not clear. The obvious answer seems to be that a greater involvement of elected politicians would reduce the chain of delegation and bring governance of international trade closer to the electorate. In practice, however, developing country delegations – even some from the larger developing countries – frequently complain that the highly technical nature of WTO negotiations means that their politicians are ill equipped to engage positively in the negotiation process. They lack the research backing and armies of assisting officials that their counterparts from developed countries enjoy. As politicians, they are also more susceptible to bilateral arm-twisting and linkages with non-trade issues than their bureaucrats. Greater involvement of elected representatives might allow greater political commitment and speedier decision-making in the WTO. But these decisions would be arrived at by exercising even greater pressure on poorly-prepared ministers or other parliamentarians from developing countries; it is therefore unlikely that such measures would improve the democratic deficit that they seek to address, especially as ministers and their populations would begin to realize the consequences of what they had signed up to. Indeed, the Uruguay Round agreements, associated problems of implementation, and the repeatedly expressed discontent of developing countries with the perceived imbalances of the Uruguay Round bargain are a product of this process.

The claim to greater participation of NGOs in WTO processes acquires even greater validity when compared against the level of private sector participation in the WTO. Wendy Dobson and Pierre Jacquet have shown the critical role played by business coalitions in the Uruguay Round. For instance, the US Coalition of Services Industries and British Invisibles played a key role in the GATS negotiations, while the Financial Leaders' Group comprising US and EU firms played a major role in the conclusion of the financial services negotiations. Similarly powerful private sector influence, such as from pharmaceutical companies, can be traced in the conclusion of the TRIPs agreement. Companies exercise this influence through direct participation in the negotiation process, especially when they are included in delegations negotiating technical issues such as telecommunications or accountancy. In contrast, representatives from civil society are seldom able to exercise comparable influence, suggesting that some alternative route to represent these interests might be in order.

In response to these demands, the WTO has made efforts to improve NGO access to its activities. Open access is available to almost all its documents on the WTO website. NGOs are allowed to present *amicus curiae* briefs in disputes brought before the Appellate Body. Through an accreditation process, it is possible for NGOs to attend Ministerial Conferences (although they are not allowed a seat at the negotiation table unless they are included as part of a national delegation). These measures effectively translate into improved external transparency, but not greater participation. A closer examination of the evidence, however, sheds considerable doubt on whether any greater participation for NGOs, or parliamentarians, will have any positive impact on improving the democratic deficit of the WTO.

Perhaps the biggest risk of opening the door to greater institutionalized NGO participation in the WTO is that it is unclear in some instances who these organizations actually represent and to whom they might be accountable. The WTO, in its current member-driven form, can at least claim to allow one vote to each member government. In the case of democracies, these representatives bear some accountability to their peoples, no matter how far removed they are from the electorate in practice. In contrast, not even the best of NGOs are democratically elected or bear any other form of legal accountability to the civil society that they claim to represent. A closer examination of NGO activity further illustrates a risk that developing countries have long anticipated, namely that many of the NGOs that actually manage to gain a voice in international forums are based in developed countries or funded by organizations in developed countries. For instance, at the Seattle Ministerial Conference – often hailed for its NGO activism – some 87% of the 738 accredited NGOs were based in developed countries. Greater direct participation by NGOs in the WTO runs the risk of tipping the balance even further away from developing countries.

This is not to say that NGOs have no role to play in relation to the WTO. But like the private sector that they sometimes seek to balance against, they need to make their inroads into the WTO via their governments or transnationally. Their role can, in fact, often turn out to be a critical one in countries or on issues where technical awareness is low. Here NGOs can serve as an invaluable research bank and assist their governments in adopting negotiating positions that assist the marginalized in the particular society. When at odds with government policy, NGOs can form some critical transnational links with other NGOs and governments. The links between Northern and Southern NGOs, and their alliance with developing country governments, were critical to the successful conclusion of the TRIPs and Public Health Declaration at the Doha Ministerial Conference. The importance of such alliances between developing country governments and certain NGOs is only likely to increase in the future.

Finally, irrespective of the reform strategy that its members eventually adopt, it is clear that the expanded mandate of the legal WTO is out of synch with the haphazard and power-political processes that go into the making of its legal rules. This discrepancy needs to be corrected. Admittedly, institutional reform that allows a greater effective voice to developing countries will result in a slower and more arduous negotiation process. But such a process may also turn out to be a longer-lasting one that would enjoy greater legitimacy, and would thereby be less disruptive to the WTO in the longer run. Without a process of institutional reform, the consequences are more troubling. If the WTO process continues to stop-start in the self-destructive manner in which it has proceeded in recent years, the developed countries might turn entirely to bilateral and regional options. The consequences would be expensive for both sides. For developed countries they would entail heightened transaction costs – an unnecessary inconvenience – and the possibility of debilitating bilateral trade wars even among themselves. But for developing countries the consequences would be devastating. It has taken them a long time to learn to operate within the multilateral forum of the GATT/WTO, and they are now finally beginning to do so with some panache through the newfound strength of their coalitions. They would find themselves exposed to unprecedented bilateral pressures from the developed countries against which they would have no institutional protection. The WTO is all that they have against the use of unmitigated power, and it is in their own interests to ensure its strength and survival.

Further reading

This list is by no means exhaustive, but is intended to assist the interested reader in following up on some of the arguments introduced in this book.

Chapter 1

For those wishing to go into the details of international trade theory, an excellent place to start is Paul Krugman and Maurice Obstfeld's textbook, *International Economics*, 4th edn. (Reading, Mass.: Addison Wesley Longman, 1997). Another accessible place to start is Paul Krugman, 'What Should Trade Negotiators Negotiate About?' (*Journal of Economic Literature*, March 1997, Vol. 35, Issue 1: 113–20). The classic case for globalization and a direct engagement with its critics can be found in Martin Wolf, *Why Globalization Works: The Case for the Global Market Economy* (New Haven: Yale University Press, 2004), and Jagdish Bhagwati, *In Defence of Globalization* (New York: Oxford University Press, 2004).

In terms of application of these theories to the GATT and the WTO, especially useful are Bernard Hoekman and Michel Kostecki, *The Political Economy of the World Trading System: The WTO and Beyond*, 2nd edn. (Oxford: Oxford University Press, 2001), and Michael Trebilock and Robert Howse, *The Regulation of International Trade*, 2nd edn. (London: Routledge, 1999).

A history of the International Trade Organization may be found in William Diebold, Jr, 'The End of the ITO' (*Essays in International Finance*, No. 16, October 1952, Princeton University, New Jersey). Robert N. Gardner provides a detailed account of Anglo-American trade diplomacy in the post-war years in his *Sterling-Dollar Diplomacy: Anglo-American Collaboration in the Reconstruction of Multilateral Trade* (Oxford: Clarendon Press, 1956). For a history of the early years of the GATT, two useful monographs are Kenneth W. Dam, *The GATT: Law and International Economic Organization* (Chicago: University of Chicago Press, 1970) and Gerard Curzon, *Multilateral Commercial Diplomacy: The General Agreement on Tariffs and Trade and its Impact on National Commercial Policies and Techniques* (London: Michael Joseph, 1965). Raymond Vernon has an interesting paper comparing the ITO and the WTO, 'The World Trade Organization: A New Stage in International Trade and Development' (*Harvard International Law Journal*, Vol. 36, No. 2, Spring 1995).

On developing countries, see Mohamed Ayoob, *The Third World Security Predicament: State-Making, Regional Conflict and the International System* (Boulder, Co.: Lynne Rienner, 1995). Among the few books written specifically on developing countries in the GATT, particularly important is Diana Tussie's work, *The Less Developed Countries and the World Trading System: A Challenge to the GATT* (London: Francis Pinter, 1985). Also see Marc Williams, *International Economic Organizations and the Third World* (New York: Harvester Wheatsheaf, 1994).

Chapter 2

On the negotiations that led to the creation of the WTO, see Gilbert R. Winham, 'The World Trade Organization: Institution-Building in the Multilateral Trade System' (*World Economy*, Vol. 21, 1998: 349–68). For the views of Sylvia Ostry, see 'The Uruguay Round North-South Grand Bargain: Implications for Future Negotiations, Political Economy of International Trade Law', University of Minnesota, September 2000; available at *http://www.utoronto.ca/cis/ostry.html*. John Croome presents a detailed study of the Uruguay Round negotiations in his

Reshaping the World Trading System: A History of the Uruguay Round
(Geneva: World Trade Organization, 1995). For a legal perspective on
the transition from the GATT to the WTO, see John H. Jackson, *The
World Trading System: Law and Policy of International Economic
Relations*, 2nd edn. (Cambridge, Mass.: MIT Press, 2002).

Chapter 3

For those interested in the intricacies of the negotiation formulae, see
Bernard Hoekman and Michel Kostecki, *The Political Economy of the
World Trading System: The WTO and Beyond*, 2nd edn. (Oxford:
Oxford University Press, 2001). John Odell provides an excellent
analysis on the process of economic negotiation in his *Negotiating the
World Economy* (Ithaca: Cornell University Press, 2000). On some of
the problems of accession, see the briefing by Oxfam International,
'Cambodia's Accession to the WTO: How the law of the jungle is applied
to one of the world's poorest countries', available at *www.oxfam.org*

Chapter 4

For an overview of all the agreements, see *Understanding the WTO*, 3rd
edn. (Geneva: WTO, August 2003); a more detailed account is provided
in Bernard Hoekman and Michel Kostecki, *The Political Economy of the
World Trading System: The WTO and Beyond*, 2nd edn. (Oxford:
Oxford University Press, 2001). See also Arvind Panagariya, 'The
Millennium Round and Developing Countries: Negotiating Strategies
and Areas of Benefit', UNCTAD and Center for International
Development, G-24 Discussion Papers Series, No. 1, March 2000. A
very useful overview and analysis of the agreements can be found in
Philip English, Bernard Hoekman, and Aaditya Mattoo (eds.),
Development, Trade and the WTO: A Handbook (Washington, DC:
World Bank, 2002). The same volume contains an excellent chapter by
J. Michael Finger and Philip Schuler entitled, 'Implementation of WTO
Commitments: The Development Challenge'. Specifically on some of
the sectors covered in this chapter, see T. Hertel and W. Martin,
'Liberalizing Agriculture and Manufactures in a Millennium Round:
Implications for Developing Countries', *World Economy*, Vol. 23, 2000:
455–70. On the expansion of the agenda of the WTO into risk

regulation, see Desmond King and Amrita Narlikar, 'International Organizations: The New Risk Regulators?' (*Political Quarterly*, July 2003). For an insightful analysis on TRIPs, see Ann Capling, 'Trading Ideas: The Politics of Intellectual Property' in *Trade Politics*, edited by Brian Hocking and Steve McGuire, 2nd edn. (London: Routledge, 2004).

Chapter 5

On the debate about legalization, see Judith Goldstein, Miles Kahler, Robert Keohane, and Anne-Marie Slaughter, *Legalization and World Politics* (Cambridge, Mass.: MIT Press, 2001) and John H. Jackson, *The World Trading System: Law and Policy of International Economic Relations*, 2nd edn. (Cambridge, Mass.: MIT Press, 2002). For an excellent account of the problems that developing countries face with the Dispute Settlement Mechanism, see Gregory Shaffer, V. Mosoti, and A. Qureshi, 'Towards a Development-Supportive Dispute Settlement System in the WTO' (*Sustainable Development and Trade Issues*, ICTSD Resource Paper No. 5, Geneva, available at *www.ictsd.org*). Also see Marc Busch and Eric Reinhardt, 'Testing International Trade Law: Empirical Studies of GATT/WTO Dispute Settlement', in *The Political Economy of International Trade Law: Essays in Honor of Robert E. Hudec*, edited by Daniel Kennedy and James Southwick (Cambridge: Cambridge University Press, 2002).

Chapter 6

The Doha documents, Cancun Declaration, and July Package can be accessed on *www.wto.org*. For some interesting anecdotes on the bilateral deals that were made at Doha, see Aileen Kwa, *Power Politics in the WTO* (Bangkok: Focus on the Global South, 2003). On the coalitions of developing countries through the Uruguay Round and leading up to the Doha Ministerial Conference, see Amrita Narlikar, *International Trade and Developing Countries: Bargaining Coalitions in the GATT and WTO* (London: Routledge, 2003). Some interesting research papers on developing countries in trade negotiations were presented at the Research Conference on Developing Countries and the Trade Negotiation Process, 6 and 7 November 2003, Palais des Nations,

Geneva; some are available at *http://www.ruig-gian.org/conf/ negocecommprogpapers.htm;* forthcoming in John Odell (ed.), *Negotiating Trade: Developing Countries in the WTO and NAFTA* (Cambridge: Cambridge University Press, 2006). Jagdish Bhagwati's book, *The World Trading System at Risk* (Princeton: Princeton University Press, 1991), was written almost fifteen years ago, but remains as relevant today on the threats to the multilateral trading system.

Chapter 7

For recent debates on institutional reform, see *Journal of International Economic Law*, September 2004. Other works cited in the chapter are: Jeffrey Schott and Jayashree Watal, 'Decision-Making in the WTO' (International Economic Policy Briefs (00–2), Washington, DC: Institute for International Economics, March 2000); Vinod Rege, 'WTO Procedures for Decision Making: Experience of Their Operation and Suggestions for Improvement' (Background Paper, Commonwealth Secretariat, 21 January 2000). Specific proposals from countries can be accessed at *www.wto.org.* For the role of the private sector in pushing for financial services liberalization, see Wendy Dobson and Pierre Jacquet, *Financial Services Liberalization in the WTO* (Washington, DC: Institute for International Economics, 1998).

Index

A

accession process 57–8, 60
accountability 134, 136
ACP (African Caribbean and
    Pacific) countries 91,
    103–4, 113, 120
Africa 46, 91, 103–4, 106, 111,
    112–13, 120, 127
African Group 113, 115
agenda setting 50, 56, 126, 130
agriculture 20, 21, 25, 50, 54,
    65, 66, 73
    Cancun Ministerial
        Conference 109, 110–11,
        114–15
    GATT 1994 67–70, 72–3, 79
    GATT exceptions 18
    ITO exception 14
    July Package 118–19
    negotiations 53
    tariff peaks 57
    WTO agreement on 26
Air Transport Services (GATS
    special agreement) 79
Alliance on Strategic Products
    and Special Safeguard
    Mechanism 112–13
Amber Box subsidies 69
amicus curiae briefs 39–40,
    136
AMS (Aggregate Measure of
    Support) 69, 70
Annecy Round (1949) 20
Anti-Dumping (ADs)
    provision 60, 75–6, 108

Appellate Body 39–40, 73, 85,
    87, 93, 94, 136
arbitration 92
Argentina 67, 73, 111
Australia 53, 67, 91, 117–21,
    128
Ayoob, Mohammed 8

B

balance of payments 13, 37, 38,
    75
Baldwin, Robert 62
Bangladesh 112
Barshefsky, Charlene 102
Bergsten, Fred 62
bilateralism 7, 10, 52, 54,
    57, 75, 85, 99, 116,
    135
Blackhurst, Richard and
    Hartridge, David 125
Blair House accord (1993) 68,
    70, 110
Blue Box subsidies 70
Bolivia 111
Botswana 115
Brazil 7, 8, 13, 68
    AIDS drugs 106
    G20 111
    GATT 18
    IPR regime 82
    July Package 53, 117–21
    as third party to disputes
        95
Bretton Woods conference
    (1944) 10
Britain 10, 13
Busch, Marc *see* Reinhardt,
    Eric and Busch, Marc

C

Cairns Group 67–9, 111
call centres 80
Cambodia 57
Canada 73
  Cairns Group 68
  GATT 19
  proposals for WTO reform
    124
  Seattle Ministerial
    Conference 101
  trade policy reviews 90
  WTO 24–5
Cancun Ministerial
  Conference (2003) 1–2,
  48, 49, 50, 53, 108, 109–21
CAP (Common Agricultural
  Policy) 18
Capling, Ann 82
Caribbean countries 7, 47, 72,
  91, 103, 120
Castillo, Carlos Perez del 48,
  110
Castillo draft 48, 49, 114
Centre William Rappard,
  Geneva 27
Chile 13, 68, 111
China 7, 9, 111
clothing 70–1, 115, 120
Colombia 68, 111
comparative advantage 2, 23,
  62, 64, 66, 76, 79, 132
compensation 6, 70, 87, 91, 97,
  115
competition policy 101, 114
complaints 73, 90–1, 93, 95–7
computer chips 25
concessions 52, 54, 57, 130

consensus 56, 124, 126, 127
  explicit 49–50, 114
  negative 32–3, 87, 92
  positive 86
  WTO decision-making and
    44–5
consultative board proposal
  124–7
consumers 5, 17, 77
contracting parties 16–17, 18,
  20, 22, 24, 25, 33
copyright 81, 83
Core Group 112, 114
Costa Rica 111
cotton 110, 115, 118
counterfeit goods 82
Countervailing Duties (CVDs)
  75, 108
Croome, John 24
Cuba 54–5, 103–4, 111, 112
cultural habits 73, 93
currency devaluation 3
customs valuation 61, 63, 72

D

Das, B. L. 56–7
decision-making procedures:
  GATT 17–18, 19
  ITO 12
  WTO 26, 43–51, 102–3, 122,
    124–7, 133–8
deficiency payments 70
delegation 35, 45, 46, 85,
  134–5
democratic deficit 100, 123,
  133–8
Derbez, Luis Ernesto 50,
  114–15

Derbez draft 112, 114
developed countries *see*
    Australia; Canada; EU;
    Japan; New Zealand;
    United States
developing countries:
  agricultural tariffs 70
  coalitions at Cancun
    Ministerial Conference
    111–13, 114, 117–18
  against consultative board
    proposal 125, 126
  defining 7–9
  dispute settlement
    mechanisms 89, 92,
    95–8
  Doha Development Agenda
    105
  and draft texts 48–9, 110
  expanding WTO mandate
    129, 137–8
  G20 111–12, 120
  GATT 17, 18–19, 21
  implementation costs 71–3,
    83, 84
  issue linkage 54–5
  ITO 13
  July Package 118–20
  and multilateral trade
    organizations 6–7
  negotiations 56–7
  principle of non-reciprocity
    29
  Seattle Ministerial
    Conference 101–2
  tariffs 64–6
  textiles 70–1
  trade in services 77,
    79

TRIMs (Trade Related
    Investment Measures)
    74
TRIPs (trade-related
    intellectual property
    rights) 71, 81–4,
    105–7
value of predictability to 6–7,
    46–7, 127
voting power 43–4
WTO 23, 25, 45
Diebold, William 14
Dillon Round (1960–61) 20
diplomacy 39, 45–51, 68,
    128–9
Dispute Settlement Body 37,
    38, 39, 40
dispute settlement
    mechanism:
  GATT 15, 17, 19, 20
  ITO 12–13
  WTO 24, 25, 32, 52, 58, 73,
    75, 86–98
Dispute Settlement
    Understanding 31, 60, 85,
    109
distribution 5, 6, 56
Dobson, Wendy and Jacquet,
    Pierre 135
Doha Development Agenda
    55, 84, 97, 99,
    102–21
Doha Ministerial Conference
    (2001) 37, 49, 67, 102–9,
    132–3, 137
  agricultural negotiations 53
  Doha Development Agenda
    102
  TRIPs 84, 107

E

economic development 12, 13, 37, 38

Economic Needs Test 79

ECOSOC (Economic and Social Council) of UN 22

Ecuador 91, 111

Egypt 54-5, 103-4, 112

El Salvador 111

employment 2, 12, 101-2, 108, 131, 132

enforcement mechanisms 5, 6, 12, 29, 33, 76

environmental issues 37, 38, 93, 103, 109, 131, 132

EU (European Union):

agriculture 18, 57, 68-9, 70, 110, 111

ban on US beef treated with hormones 73, 93

bananas regime 91

enlargement 130

GATT 19

July Package 53, 117-21

proposals for WTO reform 124

Singapore issues 48-9, 50, 101, 112, 114-15, 118

as third party to disputes 95

trade policy reviews 90

WTO 24-5

explicit consensus 49-50, 114

export-orientated growth

export subsidies 70, 111-12, 118

exports 74, 75, 91

F

Facilitators 50

Fiji 68

financial services 79, 80, 135

Finger, J. Michael and Schuler, Philip 71, 72, 73

Finland 91

'Five Interested Parties' 120

food imports 70

footwear 66

free riding 29, 52, 81

free trade, US commitment to 10, 13, 14

G

G20 111-12, 120

G90 113

Gardner, Richard 12

GATS (General Agreement on Trade in Services) 76-80

GATT 1947 60, 63, 64, 75

GATT 1994 (Multilateral Agreement on Trade in Goods) 60, 63-76, 78, 90

GATT (General Agreement on Tariffs and Trade) 15-21

Agreements *see* individual Rounds

'bicycle theory' 62

compared to WTO 30-3, 35, 36, 42, 55, 59, 86

consensus decision-making 44-5, 94

Generalized System of Preferences 29

Ministerial Conferences 36

negotiating culture of 19, 55

non-reciprocity principle 29
WTO function 23, 26, 127
gender inequality 131
General Council (WTO) 37, 38, 40, 87, 127, 132
Geneva 27, 37
Geneva Conference (1947) 15, 20
Geneva Round (1956) 20
Goldstein, Judith 85
goods 31, 32, 37, 38, 60, 63–76
government procurement 60, 101, 114
'Grand Bargain' 23, 25, 63–76, 130
'grandfather clause' 16, 28, 30–1
Green Box subsidies 69, 111, 119
Green Room meetings 17–18, 46, 55, 124
Guatemala 91, 111

H

Harbinson, Stuart 49, 109
Hartridge, David *see* Blackhurst, Richard and Hartridge, David
Havanna Charter 10–14, 15, 132
Hertel, T. and Martin, W. 70
HIV/AIDS 105–7
Hoekman, Bernard and Kostecki, Michel 4, 28, 39, 52, 63, 64, 65, 90, 95
Honduras 91
Hong Kong 128
Hull, Cordell 10

human rights 12, 131, 132
Hungary 68

I

ICITO (Interim Commission for the International Trade Organization) 16–17, 33
IMF (International Monetary Fund) 10, 24, 33, 34, 35, 43
implementation costs 71–3, 83, 102, 108
import bans 73, 93
import restrictions 63
imports 69, 70, 72, 106, 109
income inequality 131
India 7, 8, 13
    call centres relocated to 80
    Core Group 112
    Doha Ministerial Conference 109
    G20 111
    GATT 18
    IPR regime 82
    July Package 53, 117–21
    Like Minded Group 54–5, 103–4, 108
    shrimp-turtles dispute 93
    as third party to disputes 95
Indonesia 54–5, 68, 103–4, 112
industrial designs 83
industrial goods 21
industrial tariffs 65, 103
informal meetings 17–18, 39, 45–51, 55, 124
intellectual property rights 60, 62, 71, *see also* TRIPs

interest groups 39, 40
International Bank for
  Reconstruction and
  Development *see* World
  Bank
International Court of Justice
  13
international relations theory
  6–7
International Technology
  Agreement 60
investment measures 21, 31,
  32, 71, 74, 101, 114
issue linkage 54
ITO (International Trade
  Organization) 10–15, 15,
  22, 132

J

Jackson, John 24, 87, 94
Jacquet, Pierre *see* Dobson,
  Wendy and Jacquet,
  Pierre
Jamaica 72
Japan 18, 19, 69, 90
July Package (2004) 53,
  117–21

K

Kahler, Miles 85
Kennedy Round (1964–67) 19,
  20, 53, 60
Kenya 112
Keohane, Robert 85
Keynesian economics 13
Kodak vs Fuji case 96
Korea 128
Kostecki, Michel *see* Hoekman,

Bernard and Kostecki,
  Michel
Krasner, Stephen 6, 128
Krugman, Paul 3
Kwa, Aileen 103

L

labour standards 108, 131, 132
Lamy, Pascal 116, 124
Latin American countries 46,
  68, 91, 111, 112–13, 125
Lavorel, Warrant 25
LDCs (Least Developed
  Countries) 9, 37, 57, 73,
  90, 107, 113, 119
legalization 16, 30, 42, 85–6,
  92–4
linear cutting formula 53
LMG (Like Minded Group)
  54–5, 103–4, 108, 127,
  128
London Conference (1946) 13

M

Malaysia 54–5, 68, 93, 103–4,
  112
marginalization 8, 18, 19, 53,
  63, 68, 95–6
market access 61, 79, 109, 110,
  111, 113, 118, 119
Marrakesh Agreement (1994)
  2, 22, 25, 26, 32, 60, 68,
  80
  annexes to 60–84
  consensus decision-making
  44
  Dispute Settlement
  Understanding 86

international co-operation
132
Ministerial Conferences 36
voting procedures 43
WTO organizational
structure 30, 33
medicine 81, 105–7, 109, 135
Mexico 91, 95, 111, 125, 128
MFN (Most Favoured Nation)
16, 28, 51, 52, 58, 63, 64,
75, 79, 120
Ministerial Conferences 36,
37, 38, 39, 40, 127
accredited NGOs at 136
draft texts for 48–9
failure rate 99, 122, *see also
under* individual
conferences
Moore, Mike 36
Movement of Natural Persons
(GATS special agreement)
79–80
Multi-Fibre Agreement (1974)
18, 66, 71
multilateralism 5, 14, 54, 130
multinational corporations
(MNCs) 74, 132

N

NAMA (non-agricultural
market access) 109, 110,
113
national treatment rule 28, 63,
79
negative consensus 32–3, 87, 92
negotiation process:
DSB adjudication 94
GATT 17–18, 19

ITO 14
TNC 109
WTO 23, 35–6, 37, 51–7,
133–5
New Zealand 68, 91, 128
NGOs (non-governmental
organizations) 39, 100,
103, 116, 117, 127–8, 130,
134, 135–7
Nigeria 112
non-discrimination principle
15–16, 28, 29, 63, 79, 83,
90
non-reciprocity principle 19,
29
non-tariff barriers (NTBs) 18,
20, 32, 59, 60, 71, 79,
131–2
non-violation complaint 90
North Atlantic Free Trade
Agreement 79

O

Odell, John 55–6
Omnibus Trade and
Competitiveness Act
(1988) 82
one-member-one-vote 17,
43–4, 127
Ostry, Sylvia 23

P

Pakistan 54–5, 93, 103–4, 109,
112
Panagariya, Arvind 105
Panitchpakdi, Supachai 36
Paraguay 111
patents 81, 82, 83, 84, 106

Peru 111
pharmaceuticals 82, 105–7, 110, 135
Philippines 68, 111
plurilateral agreements 19, 32, 43, 60, 61
plurilateral committees 37, 38, 39
politicians 134–5
positive consensus 86
Prasidh, Cham 57
predictability 6–7, 46–7
Principal Supplier Principle (PSP) 17, 18, 45, 52–5
Prisoners' Dilemma game 4
protectionism 3, 5–6, 20, 72, 132
  non-tariff forms of 62
  and perfectionists 14
  tariffs and 64
  textile exports 18
  and WTO Agreement 26
protesters 1, 100, 122
Protocol of Provisional Application 16, 28, 30
public health 105–7, 109, 137

Q

Quad Group (US, EU, Canada and Japan) 19, 90, 103
quantitative restrictions 63, 74
quotas 18, 54, 64, 66, 67, 69, 71, 104, 111

R

raw materials 66
Reciprocal Trade Agreements Act (1945) 15

reciprocity principle 2, 5, 29, 51, 52
Red Box subsidies 69
Rege, Vinod 126
regional trade agreements 37, 38, 54, 99
Reinhardt, Eric and Busch, Marc 95
request-offer approach 54
restrictive business practices 12
retaliation 4, 6, 33, 40, 52, 73, 85, 88, 91, 92, 95, 97, 98
Ricupero, Rubens 47
Ruggiero, Renato 31, 34, 36, 100–1
rule-making 130, 134
rules 109, 127–9

S

safeguard mechanisms 75, 76, 84, 112–13, 119
sanitary and phytosanitary barriers to trade (SPS) 20, 32, 67, 71, 72–3
Schott, Jeffrey and Watal, Jayashree 125
Schuler, Philip see Finger, J. Michael and Schuler, Philip
Seattle Ministerial Conference (1999) 1, 36, 39, 46, 67, 71, 100–2, 108, 136
Senegal 9
services 20, 23, 26, 31, 32, 37, 38, 59, 60, 62, 71, 76–80, 109

Shaffer, Gregory 94, 96
Singapore 128
Singapore issues 48–9, 50, 101, 103, 108, 110, 112, 114–15, 118
Singapore Ministerial Conference (1996) 48, 50, 101
Single Undertaking 25, 31–2, 33, 54, 60, 130
Slaughter, Anne-Marie 85
Smoot-Hawley Tariff Act (1930) 3, 4
South Africa 106, 111
Southeast Asia 8, 112–13
sovereignty 72, 77
special and differential treatment (S&D) 29, 64, 108, 110, 112, 113
Special Safeguard Mechanism 113, 119
subsidies 108, 111
  agricultural 68–70
  cotton 115
  export 70, 111–12
  reduction 118–19
surveillance mechanisms 29, 33, 87
Sutherland, Peter 34
Switzerland 128

T

Tanzania 54–5, 103–4
tariff barriers 2, 3, 60
tariffs 4, 5, 53, 59, 64–7, 69, 111, 118–19, *see also* GATT
technical barriers to trade (TBT) 20, 32, 60

technology transfer 74
telecommunications 79, 80, 135
textiles 18, 20, 21, 25, 54, 66, 70–1, 104, 115, 120
Textiles Monitoring Body (WTO) 39
Thailand 68, 93, 106, 111
TNC (Trade Negotiations Committee) 109
Tokyo Round (1973–79) 19, 20, 23, 29, 31, 53, 60, 71, 86
Torquay Round (1951) 20
trade and environment 37, 38, 109
Trade Justice Movement 117
trade liberalization 2–3, 4–6, 62
Trade Policy Review Body 37, 38
Trade Policy Review Mechanism (TPRM) 29, 33, 35, 60, 89–90
trademarks 81, 83
transparency 29, 46, 61, 63, 103, 135–6
  information availability to NGOs 103
  Trade Policy Review Mechanism 89
  TRIPs agreement 83
  As part of reform agenda 127–9
TRIMs (Trade Related Investment Measures) 74
TRIPs (trade-related intellectual property rights) 20–1, 23, 26, 31, 32, 37, 38, 59, 61, 135, 137

Agreement on 80–4
AIDS and 106–7
developing countries 71,
105
Like-Minded Group and 104
TRQs (Tariff Rate Quotas) 69,
111
Truman, President Harry
11–14
trust 56–7

U

Uganda 54–5, 103–4
UN (United Nations):
Code on Conduct of
Transnational
Corporations 74
Conference on Trade and
Development 19, 29, 47,
55
ECOSOC 22
General Assembly voting
procedures 44
ITO 12, 13, 14
LDCs (Least Developed
Countries) identified by 9
unemployment 13
unilateralism 82, 85
United States:
agriculture 57, 68–9, 70, 110,
111
'carousel approach' 91
cotton subsidies 115
EU's ban on beef from 73,
93
at failure of Cancun
Ministerial Conference
115–16

GATT 19
'grandfather rights' 30–1
initial resistance to WTO 25
intellectual property rights
81
ITO 10, 11–12, 13
July Package 53, 117–21
9/11 terrorist attacks 102
patent protection 82, 106–7
Seattle Ministerial
Conference 101–2, 108
shrimp-turtles dispute 93
Smoot-Hawley Tariff Act 3,
4
as third party to disputes 95
trade in services 76, 77
trade policy reviews 90
veto power 43
Uruguay 68
Uruguay Round (1986–94) 20,
22, 23–4, 25–6, 32, 60, 70,
108
business coalitions 135
democratic deficit and 135
Dispute Settlement
Understanding 85
'Grand Bargain' 23, 25,
63–76, 130
issue linkage 54–5
'new issues' 61–2, 82
sector-by-sector negotiation
approach 53
tariff escalation 66
TRIPs 82–3

V

value-claiming/value-creating
strategy 56

Venezuela 111, 112
voluntary codes 19, 23, 24, 60, 71
voluntary export restraints (VERs) 18, 75, 77
voting procedures 17, 43–4, 127, 136

W

Watal, Jayashree *see* Schott, Jeffrey and Watal, Jayashree
Winham, Gilbert 16, 25
WIPO (World Intellectual Property Organization) 81
World Bank 10, 24, 33, 34, 35, 43, 71
WTO (World Trade Organization):
  accession process 57–8, 60
  Centre William Rappard 27
  compared to GATT 30–3, 35, 36, 42, 55, 59, 86
  consultative board proposal 124–7
  creation of 22–7
  decision-making procedures 26, 43–51, 102–3, 122, 124–7, 133–8
democratic deficit of 100, 123, 133–8
Doha Development Agenda 55, 84, 97, 99, 102–21
  inconsistencies in 26–7, 32
  informal protocols of 45–51, 55, 124
  mandate of 60–84, 129–33, 137–8
  negotiation process 23, 35–6, 37, 51–7
  NGOs participation in 135–6
  North-South antagonisms in 71–2, 110–14
  official logo of 31
  organizational structure of 33–41
  principles of 28–9
  proposals for reform of 123–9
  Secretariat 33, 35–6, *see also* Marrakesh Agreement

Z

Zambia 112
Zimbabwe 112
Zoellick, Robert 115–16